P R

Items should be returned on or before the date shown
not already requested by other borrowers may be rene
in writing or by telephone. To renew, please quote the
barcode label. To renew online a PIN is required. This
at your local library.
Renew online @ **www.dublincitypubliclibraries.ie**
Fines charged for overdue items will include postage incurred in recovery.
Damage to or loss of items will be charged to the borrower.

D0260113

Leabharlanna Poiblí Chathair Bhaile Átha Cliath
Dublin City Public Libraries Finglas Library
Brainse Fhionnghl
T: (01) 834 4906 E: finglaslibrary@dublincity.ie

Comhairle Cathrach
Bhaile Átha Cliath
Dublin City Council

Due Date	Due Date	Due Date
04 SEP 2018		2018

'In this
importa
real bu
it cover
become
David

'I have
much f
needs t
Comm

'Get Soc
shares
social",
strategy
my soci
as a bet
Interio

'I've inv
media

hands-on learning and knowledge of the wider landscape. The book covers an
introduction to the landscape, why it matters to leaders and business – as well as
practical strategy and tactics via her 90-day programme. It's a very conversational
read. In my view, *Get Social* is an absolute must for all leaders looking to
understand where we are with social and how they can get involved, if they
choose to do so.' **Claire Debney, legal strategy consultant and executive coach**

'This is an outstanding book that covers all the basics for CEOs of companies
wanting to lead their organizations on social media. This book tells you
want you need to know about the different platforms in terms of audience
and effective techniques. It has a very useful chapter to help you consider
what content to organize and how to tie in your messages with your overall

business objectives. The author underlines the fact that content isn't about SEO and keywords, so much as about the CEO being authentic and sharing what's important to them and their organization. I really found this book to be very informative and helpful, especially for CEOs wanting to improve their social media engagement and use it as a marketing tool. I found it useful how a chapter at the end brings everything together to help you put together an implementation plan over 90 days. This book is 100 per cent recommended.'
Shireen Smith LLM, Founder, Azrights, and author of *Legally Branded*

'Are you a CEO or Business Leader? We live in social times and it's time to get Social. Michelle's book takes you through why and how to get on and master social media. Providing both a strategy and a 90-day plan, it will certainly get you started on your social media journey. Your only risk, of course, is not being there.' **Tim Hughes, Co-Founder, Digital Leadership Associates, and author of *Social Selling***

'A compelling business strategy book for leaders on social media. How refreshing. A valuable resource packed with rich data, smart frameworks and sound logic. In the world of social media, business leaders don't need to be technically proficient to be a powerful influence but they do need to be uniquely informed. Michelle Carvill helps leaders unlock their untapped source of competitive advantage and how to best communicate it to employees, customers and shareholders.' **John Dodds, Senior Member, The Sharp End LLC**

'Having worked with Michelle, it's clear to see that *Get Social* brings her practical approach to its pages. For those leaders and business owners struggling to get to grips with how they show up on social media, this book provides the perfect step-by-step solution.' **Michelle Alcock, Managing Director, Teknos**

'I have shared and recommended Michelle's previous books with a number of my clients and contacts; given the depth of content, there really is no other need for them to read anything else on the subject. I was therefore excited to read *Get Social*, and I wasn't disappointed. With its practical 90-day planning aspect and focus on personal branding for leaders, thought leadership and effective communication, it provides a trusted go-to resource for any leader. My proof copy is already well thumbed!' **Alison Relf, Director, Taylor Alden**

'This is a great read on a vast subject that affects us all both personally and in our business lives. As well as the layout, what I like about this book is the fact that it accepts "we are all in some way using social media" and focuses more on "how we get more from social media". The strategic approach of *Get Social* really makes you think about the future of social media and its impact on your business and personal life, especially with the 90-day strategy plan. *Get Social* highlights the point that social media isn't something that you can just dip in and out of but more that one must now make it part of one's business planning. I was shocked to read that social media users are still increasing at a rate of 1 million people per day. This only adds to the importance of strategy – I have said that all people need a VIMS (Valued Individual Marketing Strategy) to ensure they get the best and what they want from social media, as it is a powerful tool that can either work for you or against you.

A really interesting book that all business leaders, marketing individuals and strategic planners should take the time to read – after all, as the book explains, *content* is key!' **Steve Preston, Managing Director, Heat Recruitment**

'Michelle has written a very practical guide for business leaders to get the most out of using social platforms which will benefit both them and their companies. A jargon-free step-by-step approach suitable for the novice and social superstar. Read this book, and be prepared to get started – immediately.' **Jasper Martens, VP Marketing, PensionBee**

'*Get Social* shows how social media can create value in many ways across all areas of an organization, debunking the idea that it is a "nice to have" or exclusively for the marketing department. The book has a great balance between the strategic rationale for leaders to invest in social media personally and within their organization, and practical advice on how to most effectively use the different platforms.' **Nathan Bray, Co-Founder and Chief Marketing Officer, ConnectMyApps**

Brainse Fhionnglaise   Finglas
T: (01) 834 4906 E: finglaslibrary@dublincity.ie

'*Get Social* is the perfect book for busy CEOs and business leaders who want to use social media to deliver tangible results for their organizations. Whether you want to build greater trust with your customers, increase employee engagement or promote yourself as a thought leader, this book will give you the proven strategies, tactics and time-saving shortcuts you need.

Punctuated with inspirational examples from some of the world's most successful social CEOs, and culminating in a practical step-by-step 90-day implementation plan, this is a book that will prompt even the busiest or most sceptical business leaders to embrace social media with confidence.

As a digital marketing consultant, there are very few people I would trust to talk to my clients about social media. Michelle is one of them and this book proves why.' **David Miles, CEO, The PPC Machine, digital marketing consultant, trainer and author**

'When it comes to social media, business leaders are great at talking the talk, but few ever carry through. Michelle's new book, *Get Social*, tackles this problem head on with a detailed step-by-step process to follow. Her 90-day planning system ensures your social media is effective and purposeful, not just a box-ticking exercise. Best of all, she demonstrates first-hand how it's done with interviews from industry heavy hitters that include John Legere, CEO of T-Mobile, and Brian J Dunn, former CEO of Best Buy.

If you're looking to build a deeper relationship with your online audience, this should be your first port of call.' **Danny Bermant, Founder and Director, Inbox Express, and CIM trainer**

'My clients often ask me whether they should have a social media profile. My response is to ask them whether they have explored the benefits and implications for them and their organization? Nine out of ten times, their answer is "no". *Get Social* is for any senior executive still asking themselves (and others) this question.' **Laura Hayes, leadership and business coach**

'Having worked with Michelle for a number of years, her latest book brings together her learning, insights and knowledge. A must for all leaders interested in getting to grips with social media and communicating effectively in this modern age.' **Robert Harding, Founder, Robert Harding World Photography**

'This is a great book for any business leader considering how to establish or enhance their social media presence, providing tangible and actionable advice on how to do this. Most CEOs know they should be doing it, but often struggle to think of authentic ways to engage with their customers. I think Michelle has done a great job of articulating how to make this happen. Utilizing social media effectively and building the personal brand of our CEO is something which is high on our agenda at the moment, and should be for any forward-thinking organization.' **Mark Finlay, M&A and Strategy Director, Moneypenny**

'Finally, a book that provides leaders with not just with the "why" but also the "how" social media can generate ROI across all areas of the business – whilst also equipping them with the tools and knowledge to personally take digital transformation for their business to the next level.' **Claire Walker, Group Digital Content Manager, global IT recruitment firm**

GET SOCIAL

Social media strategy and tactics for leaders

MICHELLE CARVILL

Withdrawn From Stock
Dublin Public Libraries

Leabharlanna Poiblí Chathair Baile Átha Cliath
Dublin City Public Libraries

KoganPage

Publisher's note

Every possible effort has been made to ensure that the information contained in this book is accurate at the time of going to press, and the publishers and authors cannot accept responsibility for any errors or omissions, however caused. No responsibility for loss or damage occasioned to any person acting, or refraining from action, as a result of the material in this publication can be accepted by the editor, the publisher or the author.

First published in Great Britain and the United States in 2018 by Kogan Page Limited

Apart from any fair dealing for the purposes of research or private study, or criticism or review, as permitted under the Copyright, Designs and Patents Act 1988, this publication may only be reproduced, stored or transmitted, in any form or by any means, with the prior permission in writing of the publishers, or in the case of reprographic reproduction in accordance with the terms and licences issued by the CLA. Enquiries concerning reproduction outside these terms should be sent to the publishers at the undermentioned addresses:

2nd Floor, 45 Gee Street
London
EC1V 3RS
United Kingdom

c/o Martin P Hill Consulting
122 W 27th St, 10th Floor
New York, NY 10001
USA

4737/23 Ansari Road
Daryaganj
New Delhi 110002
India

www.koganpage.com

© Michelle Carvill, 2018

The right of Michelle Carvill to be identified as the author of this work has been asserted by her in accordance with the Copyright, Designs and Patents Act 1988.

ISBN   978 0 7494 8255 8
E-ISBN   978 0 7494 8256 5

British Library Cataloguing-in-Publication Data

A CIP record for this book is available from the British Library.

Library of Congress Cataloging-in-Publication Data

Names: Carvill, Michelle, 1969- author.
Title: Get social : social media strategy and tactics for leaders / Michelle
   Carvill.
Description: 1st Edition. | New York, NY : Kogan Page Ltd, [2018] | Includes
   index.
Identifiers: LCCN 2018002908 (print) | LCCN 2018001711 (ebook) | ISBN
   9780749482565 (ebook) | ISBN 9780749482558 (pbk.)
Subjects: LCSH: Online social networks in business. | Leadership.
Classification: LCC HM742 (print) | LCC HM742 .C3577 2018 (ebook) | DDC
   302.30285–dc23
LC record available at https://lccn.loc.gov/2018002908

Typeset by Integra Software Services Pvt Ltd, Pondicherry
Print production managed by Jellyfish
Printed and bound by CPI Group (UK) Ltd, Croydon, CR0 4YY

References to websites (URLs) were accurate at the time of writing. Neither the author nor Kogan Page is responsible for URLs that may have expired or changed since the manuscript was prepared.

CONTENTS

ACKNOWLEDGEMENTS

My sincere thanks and gratitude to:

The CEOs and leaders (John Legere, Caron Bradshaw, Kevin Burrowes, Brian J Dunn, Shaa Wasmund, Steve Tappin, Kevin Roberts, Gordon Beattie and Dr Sam Collins) who 'get social' and very generously agreed for me to share their viewpoints. It has been a pleasure chatting with them and their teams (albeit largely digitally).

Roland Deiser for support and allowing me to share his research around leadership and social literacy.

Géraldine Collard, my commissioning editor, for patience and steer. *Get Social* has far more 'dots joined up' thanks to her influence.

Friends and online tribes for constant encouragement and humour.

My two beautiful girls for their maturity and understanding, giving me 'guilt free' weekends to write – and for cuddles and cups of tea along the way.

And last, but certainly not least, huge gratitude and love to my husband, Kevin, my understated rock, who lovingly kept all the wheels spinning in my book-writing absence.

Introduction

Not sure if this book is for you?

I often hear people referring to social media and the related channels and tools as being 'new' and emerging – and how imperative it is that businesses and people 'catch up'. Adapt or die.

But actually, if we think about the pace of change over the past 20 years – in the context of our continuously advancing technological climate – these channels, many of which emerged 10–15 years ago, are actually really quite established.

I started experimenting with social media channels for business purposes in late 2008, so by the time this book is published that will be almost 10 years ago.

As a marketer, with a natural interest in customer experience, complaining behaviour and service recovery, I regarded social media platforms as channels that afforded everyone the opportunity to engage directly in real conversations with brands and businesses. From a service delivery perspective, channels that no brand or business could hide away from, with automated phone queuing systems or auto-responder communications.

Therefore, initially, I was less enamoured with the creative, fun, entertaining and more marketing-led aspects of social media channels, and far more interested in the real-time, people-to-people connection they enabled. In my viewpoint, in those early days, social media channels provided an exciting platform that was no doubt going to be the catalyst to revolutionizing service delivery levels, ensuring brands were being accountable for their 'brand promises', via first-hand, direct conversations with customers. Thus, raising the level of transparency, authenticity and accountability.

As the years have evolved, one such aspect of social media has indeed been the improved 'real world, real time', authentic warts-and-all customer service aspect. Those brands that have pledged to 'get social' have often seen continued loyalty for having direct conversations with consumers. Of course, for many, it has not all been plain sailing and a lot of lessons have been learnt along the way. Many can be found in the entertaining book, *Great Brand Blunders* (2014) by Rob Gray.

A quick look at pretty much every supermarket's social media accounts will uncover that the majority have a 'Twitter' customer support persona. This continues with airlines; rail services; major retailers – Ikea, M&S, Amazon; service providers – UPS, Airbnb, Xbox; long-standing brands – Coca-Cola, Nike; governments, politicians, world leaders, the Pope – the list goes on and on. In fact, now in 2018, if a brand, business or person of influence doesn't have any social media presence, it is deemed highly unusual.

Have we reached the 'tipping point' where social media activity is now totally accepted as a valid strategic endeavour for brands and businesses? I suspect we have.

Over the past 10 years, as a consultant training people and businesses in social media, and assisting businesses in understanding how it fits into their strategic endeavours, I have personally witnessed a significant shift in both perception and engagement.

As with all new channels, initially there was mighty scepticism. In many cases, when marketing or communication team members who were keen to integrate social media into their activities invited me in to meet with chief executive officers (CEOs) and leaders to assist their case, it was often more of an inquisition than a fact-finding mission.

Conversations focused around 'convince me', 'prove to me' and 'show me the evidence', coupled with a huge reluctance to open up the doors and let the outside in. One of the most commonly asked questions I received was: 'What if someone says something awful about us on social media?' My retort was always the same: 'What if they already are, and you know nothing about it?'

Jump forward 10 years and here we are today: brands and businesses have adopted the channels and 'being social' is now business as usual. Social media adoption is mainstream.

Social media is not only a part of how we communicate and consume day-to-day (whether that's a good thing or a bad thing, it's a real thing), but a means for political advancement, charitable outreach, worldwide community development, policing and many other aspects (both positive and negative). Social media activity is now firmly woven into the fabric of our everyday lives.

Today the questions I get asked are less around 'prove to me this stuff works' but rather, 'We're doing this, but are we doing everything as well as we could be?'

Many years ago, I recall reading an article from Cisco, which today, I cannot actually find reference to. The article was forecasting how social media would likely impact our world and our business environments. I recall reading that CEOs of the future would be those who were the most 'socially' enabled. Those who were not only demonstrating all the usual gifts and skills of being an adept leader, but above and beyond that, those who were adopting new ways of leading by having authentic and transparent conversations with their employees and customers.

In a world where the majority of consumers are now engaged with social media, it is perhaps surprising to learn that comparatively only a small percentage of CEOs currently participate in social media – and for those who do, the activity is often more of a PR one rather than authentic conversations.

My own experience supports this lack of the 'social leader'. When I keynoted at a workshop with LinkedIn for leaders early in 2017, I realized that, of the 50 leaders in the room, only a handful were themselves 'social', yet social media was something each of their businesses fully participated in.

My 'why' or reason for writing this book comes from a desire to provide CEOs, leaders and aspiring leaders with a highly in-depth understanding of how and where social media fits into the bigger picture both strategically and tactically – and to provide practical tools and resources to assist any reader to be inspired to 'get social'.

Early on in the book we will build the context of why engaging on social media matters for you. And we'll explore research, statistics and adoption rates in more detail throughout Chapters 1 and 2.

We'll then move quickly into the practical side of things, addressing the 'leader's social toolkit' in Chapter 3, where we'll run through the social media channels and consider tips and tactics that are relevant for you in a leadership capacity.

Chapter 4 is all about content and, again, we're not just going to talk about what you could be doing; to keep things practical and useful we'll work through exercises and aspects related to mapping out an effective content plan, covering the role content plays for you as a 'social' leader, how to create content that creates connection, useful content tips to optimize your social media activity, and creating a compelling and balanced content plan.

Chapter 5 is where we look at your social media strategy – determining your purpose and your why. Why it makes sense to align your personal activity with business objectives, how to define your personal objectives and personal brand, determining objectively driven return-on-investment (ROI) metrics and simple tactics for practical execution, understanding and measuring progress.

Chapter 6 is where we'll address the wider context and look at how social technologies in a broader capacity are being integrated within organizations – and the reasons for and benefits of doing so. By exploring how social media fits in across your organization and how it can map into current technologies, we will look at some frameworks and benchmarks so that you can 'test' how your organization measures up and, importantly, I'll bring this back to you, and what this means for you in your role as a leader.

Chapter 7 is where all the exercises, challenges and practicalities of *Get Social* are brought together, culminating in the creation of 'your 90-day personal social media strategy and plan'.

Finally, Chapter 8 introduces you to CEOs and leaders who generously shared their insights with me, summarizing key findings. It is a teaser introduction to the Appendix, where you will find full interviews with nine active social CEOs, each doing their own thing on social media.

What you will not get from this book is masses of theoretical business school-style business models and worldly discussion of why 'being social' matters. Whilst reading the stats, facts, case studies and interviews throughout this book may spearhead your desire to get involved with social media, it is not designed to 'persuade' you to do so (although it is likely to do that), but rather to assist those who are either curious or keen to learn how best to practically 'get social'.

What you will get from this book, therefore, is a highly practical overview of where we are with social media – and, if you want to embrace it, tried and tested practical tools providing you with a tangible and accessible roadmap to do so. Intelligently, courageously and authentically.

From a resource perspective, I will draw from my own experience of training, consulting, implementing programmes and coaching leaders. As evidenced, I will also pull in real-world practical case studies from CEOs and leaders who really do 'get social'.

Time, of course, is a precious resource – and 'being social' does not mean you have to personally do everything or be glued to the channels 24/7. But as a CEO or leader you are the heart and the brains of the organization; your role is about keeping the organization thinking and breathing. Research (which we will delve into in more detail in Chapter 2) identifies that employees (70 per cent) and consumers (80 per cent) have increased trust in CEOs who are transparent and vocal. Being a 'social' CEO can create multiple benefits, including better communications, improved brand image, increased transparency and greater employee morale – all of which help to increase leadership effectiveness.

Despite these benefits, many leaders are still hesitant to adopt social media. For many leaders 'being social' is marred by a view that it's all about sharing pictures of their breakfast in the morning. There is a huge 'so what' factor to overcome in order to assist in providing the proof that being social has bottom-line benefits. To that endeavour, to assist with 'social proof', we'll hear viewpoints and advice from CEOs and leaders who are already out there and leading the way.

As stated, this book is for the curious cats, the ones who may be sitting on the rooftops already keen to take the leap but have reservations and concerns around making a complete hash of it.

Within the pages we'll push through the nonsense and irrelevant noise on social media and showcase the merits of relevant social media conversations and the insights that can be gleaned, as well as what leaders can do with those insights for the greater good of their organization.

Brainse Fhionnglaise   Finglas Library
T: (01) 834 4906 E: finglaslibrary@dublincity.ie

I have endeavoured to keep the practical content as accessible as possible and have, therefore, made no assumptions about the level of knowledge that readers may have around social media adoption, growth, channels or best practice.

Please also note that my writing style is very much 'conversational'. I've been blogging for around 10 years now and I personally find that books and blogs I read make so much more sense when written as the author speaks. You will find the tone within this book – whilst at all times professional – relaxed, conversational and, hopefully, totally relatable.

To complement the contents of *Get Social*, I have also created the online hub GetSocial.site, which is a dedicated website where you will find the resources outlined within these pages for you to visit and download as relevant.

I'll also curate and share articles, stats and research to the blog on the GetSocial.site too, with the intention that the site, as well as the book, will become useful resources for you to dip in and out of.

To chat directly you will find me on Twitter @michellecarvill and LinkedIn/michellecarvill. I encourage and welcome you to engage – I'm always happy to answer questions and chat.

For those looking for inspiration, I hope the research, stories and advice as to what others are doing provides you with that – and for those looking to take action, I hope I've given you enough to help you 'get social' both in spirit and practically.

Enjoy.

01
Leading a business in a socially connected world

G iven this book is aimed at you, the leader, I wanted to start off by focusing directly on what being a leader in a socially connected world means for you.

This chapter aims to provide you with insights on where social media for you as a leader fits in, why it matters and the impact that 'being social' can have.

In fact, before we start, here's my list of some of the clear benefits. Social media:

- enables you to tune in and listen in 'real time' to your customers, your employees and what's happening in your sector;
- enables you to share your viewpoint in an authentic and conversational way;
- enables you to defend, speak up and mitigate misconceptions;
- enables you to share your values and your brand's values.

As we go through the book, you'll hear what other leaders feel are the benefits of being on social media channels – and I'll endeavour to demonstrate all of the above with real-world examples.

My viewpoint and, therefore, the stance in this book, considers that social media, as well as offering you highly practical channels to assist you with driving your business, reaches way beyond the practical application of 'being social on social networks' – and rather is enmeshed within the range of technologies that are fast becoming 'social' business as usual.

Whilst the focus of this book is to enable you to develop your own social media strategy and tactics, it would be a disservice not to discuss the breadth and depth of social technologies, to equip you with enough compelling context to motivate you to take action and build social media strategies, tactics and activity into your already busy life. After all, leadership in a fast-changing, highly technological complex world is no easy task.

Kevin Roberts, former CEO of Saatchi & Saatchi, in his engaging book, *64 Shots: Leadership in a crazy world* succinctly states: 'We live in a VUCA world. Volatile. Uncertain. Complex. Ambiguous. VUCA is a military acronym that has penetrated business speak. It recognizes that leading a business has become like flying through an asteroid field' (Roberts, 2016).

When I read that paragraph in Kevin Roberts's book it really resonated. Whilst technological development is deemed highly positive in many respects, getting your head around it in a comprehensive way, and then keeping on top of the pace of change, can feel very overwhelming.

In short, business has changed more quickly and dramatically over the past 20 years than at any time since the Industrial Revolution. The good (or the bad) news is that this rapid change is only going to continue.

There is already a sea change in the growing number of CEOs and leaders embracing social technologies within business and also taking to the social media stage. 'Social leadership' is inevitable – as cited in BrandFog's (2016) 'CEOs, Social Media and Brand Reputation' survey:

> More and more CEOs are embracing social media as a leadership tool. Social media enables C-suite leaders to become more prominent, accessible and identifiable within their industry. We expect that in the next 18–24 months, social engagement at the executive level will become the norm across many organizations globally. (BrandFog, 2016)

As the saying goes, 'The time to repair the roof is when the sun is shining.' So if you too are feeling a little overwhelmed and are not as au fait as you feel you need to be around becoming a 'social leader', then this chapter provides you with compelling findings and insights to evidence where social media fits in – not just personally, but across the business.

As stated in the Introduction (and this is a message I'll keep returning to), the purpose of this book, call it my mission if you prefer, is to provide you with a practical guide to getting social, equipping you with context, know-how and practical application.

My objective is that you get to the end of this book feeling that you know exactly what you are doing on social media and, importantly, why you are doing it – equipped and confident to either get started if you are standing on the sidelines at the moment, or indeed reinvent your current activity.

What you will learn from this chapter

- How business is changing thanks to our socially connected world.
- The opportunities social media provides to you as a 'social leader'.
- The shift in consumer expectation and the rise of the belief-driven buyer.
- How social media helps you to strengthen the consumer–brand relationship.

How digital is transforming business

There's no doubt about it. Ten years ago, the world was a simpler place.

Technologies that are fast becoming part of our everyday lives would, 10 years ago, have been more aligned with the realms of science fiction or fantasy: straight out of a film studio.

Right now we have intelligent cars (remember KITT in *Knight Rider*? If you don't, google it), talking tech within the household ('Alexa, what's the weather going to be like today?') and smart-energy appliances that organize the heating and cooling of your home, whether you are home or away. You can also now hire a robot programmed to be a receptionist at a comparable salary cost of £26,000 (Howes, 2017).

Current and emerging technologies such as artificial intelligence (AI), augmented reality (AR), virtual reality (VR), the internet of things (IoT), robotics, 3-D printing, blockchain and drones are fast becoming business as usual.

It's not just your typical high-tech businesses embracing these technologies. Adoption is widespread, covering manufacturing, engineering, retail, energy, media, health care, agriculture, education, government, financial services and transportation – to name but a few.

Aligned with all these new and emerging technologies is, of course, the sheer volume of data and insights they capacitate. The 'big data' aspect continues to prove challenging for many organizations. After all, it's one thing collecting the enormous amount of data available to us; it's another to organize, prioritize and interpret it in a way that facilitates useful insights and timely competitive advantage.

Is it any wonder, then, that digital transformation and all it entails is a hot topic on the agenda of many C-suite discussions?

For the past 10 years, PwC has been measuring digital IQ. In April 2017, they released their 10-year summary report, 'A decade of digital: keeping pace with transformation'.

In 2007, when their survey started, just 33 per cent of executives said their CEO was 'a champion for digital' (PwC, 2017). Over the past 10 years that number has climbed to 68 per cent today. In fact, today it would be challenging to find an organization, regardless of size or sector, that does not consider digital technology to be an integral element of their business strategy and operations.

From a social media perspective, when the digital IQ survey began back in 2007, Twitter, LinkedIn, YouTube and Facebook were very much the new kids on the block – still figuring out how to create commercial impact. However, a decade later, and as we'll explore in greater detail in Chapter 2, these social technologies, along with others and together with mobile technology, have totally evolved the way we humans communicate. Whether we buy into it or not, social technologies now totally pervade our lives and already significantly impact how humans and machines work together.

Whilst the PwC 10-year report highlights the increased awareness of the business value associated with new technology adoption, it also highlights that companies 'have not adapted quickly enough to stay ahead of constant change' (PwC, 2017).

In fact, confidence in 'staying ahead', rather than continuing to increase, has dropped. In PwC's recent survey, only 52 per cent of companies rated their digital IQ as strong. However, in their previous survey it was 67 per cent and, in the one before that, 66 per cent. What is evident from these latest findings is that there has been a marked decline.

Aligned with the drop in confidence reported in the PwC report it is interesting to turn also to the Edelman Trust Barometer at this point (Edelman, 2017b). Their 2017 study findings showcase that the general global population's trust in four key areas – business, government, non-government organizations (NGOs) and media – has declined recently too. This is a trend unseen since they started tracking trust amongst these segments in 2012. Their latest findings report that, whilst trust is down generally across the board, from a business landscape perspective, trust in CEOs is at an all-time low of just 37 per cent.

In summary, the findings from these reports highlight two key challenges: 1) keeping up with the pace and breadth of digital and technological continuous advances is becoming more of a challenge for leaders; 2) leaders are not doing enough to engender trust and build stronger relationships with customers. Admittedly, the above studies focus on larger corporations – but these same challenges filter down as very real issues for small businesses and even micro-businesses.

I have met a significant number of people who, whilst very competent in their areas of expertise, regardless of the size of their organization, feel at the very least overwhelmed with the pace of change and keeping up with technology. The two key aspects of 1) keeping up with the pace of change, and 2) building stronger relationships with customers, are very real challenges for all leaders.

In the context of social media being part of our digital transformation, turning to the first challenge of keeping up with change, whilst it is encouraging that more CEOs and leaders are starting to take to the social media stage, recent research from a variety of sources suggests that the shift to becoming a 'social leader' is not moving fast enough.

In 2010, Weber Shandwick launched a research study, 'Socializing Your CEO'. Over the past seven years they have been tracking an index measuring the online presence of CEOs on social networks and their level of social media engagement.

The 2017 findings (Weber Shandwick, 2017) showcase that whilst CEO presence on social networks is at first encouraging, showing growth, with 92 per cent of the US top 50 Fortune 500 CEOs having a social media presence, only 22 per cent of CEOs have actually engaged (defined as having written a post or responded) in the past 12 months.

CEO.com, in association with business management software company Domo, have also been reviewing the social media habits of all Fortune 500 companies since 2013 (CEO.com, 2016). Whilst they again found that the number of CEOs on the platforms was gradually increasing, their report highlighted that among the Fortune 500 CEOs, 60 per cent still had no social media presence at all and, on some platforms, CEO involvement was on the decline.

Why does being social as a leader matter for you?

Thanks to social networks and mobile technologies (as we will explore in greater detail in Chapter 2), social media networks now pervade the lives of literally billions of people.

From a business perspective, the majority of organizations have embraced the necessity of having a social media presence. Let's face it, you cannot even pick up your pack of coffee in the morning without seeing an array of social media icons emblazoned on the packaging, encouraging you to 'engage' one way or another. Regardless of whether the focus is business to business (B2B) or business to consumer (B2C), social media channels are now largely accepted as a natural part of the suite of channels used to communicate with audiences.

Coming back to you, then, the CEO or leader within your organization: why does it matter whether you get involved or not? Surely it is the remit of your digital, marketing, communications or customer service teams (if you have them!) to optimize the array of social channels for the overall good of the business. Right?

Well, actually, perhaps that is not so right. In fact, let's take a few steps back to the second challenge identified above – the all-important 'trust' factor and the development of stronger relationships with customers.

For the last four years, as cited earlier, BrandFog has been studying the role that social media plays in the development of industry leadership, brand trust and brand reputation. Their 2016 survey findings showcase the following (BrandFog, 2016) for the people surveyed:

- 82 per cent were more likely to trust a company whose leadership team engages with social media;
- 78 per cent would prefer to work for a company whose leadership is active on social media;
- 81 per cent believe that CEOs who engage in social media are better equipped than their peers to lead companies in this digital world;
- 85 per cent believe that CEOs can use social media channels to improve engagement with employees;
- 86 per cent rated CEO social media engagement as either somewhat important or very important or mission critical.

What shines through to me from the studies and survey findings is that whilst there is evidence showcasing the value for leaders to 'get social', many 'leaders' (and yes, that could be you too) are not really on board.

Fake social

As outlined in the study findings, many leaders have indeed set up channels and, in some cases, are forced to do so. But they are not really doing anything with them. In fact, I experienced this a lot myself when researching case studies for this book. Keen to interview active social CEOs and leaders to get a real-world viewpoint, I took to the mighty Google and social media channels to uncover the most social CEOs to add to my hit list.

Initially, I was hugely encouraged as I was able to find profiles for a large number of CEOs and senior leaders. However, a few seconds perusing their platforms told me everything I needed to know. Sadly, it wasn't unusual for the most 'recent post' to have been written many months or, in some cases, even many years, ago.

Of course, if you're just there as a bystander, paying lip service to being social, it can look a whole lot worse. After all, if a customer, supplier, partner, journalist or stakeholder sees that you have a social profile and turns to that channel to open an authentic conversation with you, or to ask a question, only to be met with total silence, then what message does that convey? In fact, in some cases, particularly if the initiator is disgruntled in some way, the radio silence is only likely to add fuel to the fire.

Let's say the initiator is not disgruntled (after all, there is just as much positive sentiment out on the social networks); let's instead say they are simply taking the time to thank you or your organization for the great work you are doing. Again, in an age where the consumer expects genuine engagement, a zero response is disappointing to say the least. From a 'building deeper relationships' with your customer perspective, it really is totally missing an opportunity.

Similarly, if a partner, potential client, customer or journalist is looking to seek your opinion on something, and they notice that the last Twitter update was May 2012, again – think about the signal that sends out.

I started but then I 'gave up'/'had more pressing priorities'/'couldn't make the time'/'this channel really isn't for the likes of me'/'I'm only on here because I've been forced to be on here'. Regardless of the reasons, others will be forming their own opinions and filling in the blanks for you.

Starting something and leaving it hanging is not the sentiment of a committed leader looking to deepen relationships and engage with customers. My advice has always been, and continues to be, that it is better not to make any attempt to be social at all if the action and sentiment is not genuine.

A bit of coaching from me

Okay, so right now is not the time to say, 'Well, that's me then, Michelle – my sentiment isn't genuine and so it's better that I don't make any attempt to get social.' Too early for that I'm afraid. After all, we're only in Chapter 1. Stick with me. To keep you on track, here's a quick little YES/NO exercise:

Do you want to engender more trust for yourself, your business or your brand?	YES/NO
Do you want to improve engagement with your employees/ teams?	YES/NO
Do you want to improve engagement with your customers/ stakeholders?	YES/NO
Do you want to be seen as a 'current' leader?	YES/NO

If you answered YES to any one of the four questions above – then we're all good. If you possibly answered NO to all – then, I'm afraid I don't believe you. Read on…

Getting social really means getting social

The reality of being a social leader is that you are opening yourself up to authentic, transparent and, depending on how you want to manage social, potentially frequent, communications. You are fundamentally opening the doors to 'being social'.

This doesn't mean that you have to broadcast your every move, 24/7, sharing what you are having for breakfast and continuing a running commentary throughout the day – although you could do that if it met your objectives and was part of your planned engagement tactics (more on tactics in Chapter 4). But it does mean that you are making a commitment to being out there, perhaps via a range of public platforms, enabling you to be both accessible to your audiences and also to tune into the landscape you operate within.

Why bother?

Well, let's just reiterate some of the previous research findings. Being social:

- engenders trust;
- builds brand engagement;
- builds employee engagement;
- keeps you tuned in to current sentiment;
- safeguards reputation management.

Barometer, microphone and scout

To explore further reasons to be social I have interviewed a number of CEOs and leaders. You will find more about them and key findings in Chapter 8, and their full stories in the Appendix. I will continue to add stories and useful references to the GetSocial.site too. You will also find snippets from conversations throughout the chapters in this book.

In one interview with Brian J Dunn, former CEO of Best Buy and renowned 'social CEO' early adopter, he told me:

> ### For me, social media acted as barometer, microphone and scout
>
> **Barometer**   Giving real-time feedback on public opinion… not statistically accurate, but typically directionally accurate. A great way to take the consumers' temperature on any given topic in relation to your business and an interesting data point on your competitors.
>
> **Microphone**   Allows you to speak directly to your customers and your employees. When you can respond directly to help expedite resolution or provide explanation it goes a long way to personalizing the experience. It is evidence that someone is listening and that you care enough to listen. It also provides a platform to recognize business units (stores and dot-coms) for excellence in execution. As CEO at Best Buy, I would frequently tweet about good store visits and market visits.
>
> **Scout**   A great place to see how new trends, technologies and strategies are taking hold. It helps you see around corners.

Brian offers a number of practical uses, I'm sure you will agree. Why is it, then, that whilst there is compelling evidence and a considerable number of stories and case studies showcasing the potential rewards for leaders to 'get social', so few have taken the genuine plunge?

Common challenges

The three common challenges cited as reasons that leaders and CEOs are not personally diving in and 'getting social' are the following:

- **Time** – '*I don't have the time.*' CEOs and leaders are just too busy to build in the time to 'do' social media.

- **ROI** – '*What's the ROI?*' As a leader the focus is on growing and developing a successful business and optimizing ROI. Depending on how you view 'social', some aspects of social media activity seem to initially offer intangible return. Measuring the immediate and longer-term bottom-line impact of hits on a YouTube video or engagement on a blog post or LinkedIn Pulse article is not that simple. The tangible returns often are not clear and may be difficult to extract.

- **Training** – '*I don't "get" social.*' '*I'm not equipped to be social.*' CEOs and leaders often feel a bit out of the loop when it comes to social media. Often they have not had any coaching or training in social media best practices and therefore do not feel competent to take the reins.

All three of these challenges pose very real issues for busy leaders. But let's also consider the very real, and rather larger, fourth factor: the 'fear' factor. Fear is a big challenge for all of us:

- What if I say something wrong/controversial/stupid?

- What if my message gets taken out of context?

- What it I upset key partners?

- What if our share price dives?

- What have I got to say that is interesting?

- What if no one is listening?

These, and many more variations, are the very same 'barriers to entry' that I have heard personally over the years from the business owners, CEOs and leadership teams I have coached and trained.

If you are reading this book, and at this point nodding your head, as these are your sentiments too, then fear not, all is not lost. In fact, it's good news.

It's good news that you have picked up this book and that you are, at the very least, exploring how to 'get social'. It's even better news that, throughout the following chapters, I am going to tackle each one of these very credible objections and challenges and provide you with highly practical answers and workable solutions for each.

Remember, my purpose for writing this book is not only to help you feel fully equipped and confident to step outside of your comfort zone, but to actually have you leaping out of it, as you become excited by the potential that 'getting social' can provide to you.

But for now, considering the reasons as to why social matters, and the reasons why leaders are reticent to 'get social', let's further build on reasons to be social and bring our attention to how our socially connected world is impacting the all-important customer.

The age of the co-creating, belief-driven all-important customer

As outlined in the Introduction, my initial excitement about the social media channels and rules of play focused more on the 'calling out' of organizations to genuinely have to 'walk the talk'. In essence, less talk of 'listening to the customer' and more action.

As a marketer, over the years I have probably driven many of my clients, colleagues and peers a little bit crazy with my obsession with a 'customer first' perspective. But realistically, for the majority of organizations, a business without customers is not really a business. For those organizations that challenge this view, internal customers still figure. Therefore, what other obsession should there be?

Thanks to so-called efficiencies and automated ways of managing customers, over the past 20 years dealing directly with customers has fast become a rarity. Call centres (and in many cases, outsourced call centres that feel totally disconnected from the brand), reference or account numbers instead of names, call efficiency systems – 'you are being held in a queue' 'we care about you but we're busy right now'; 'press 2 for sales, 3 for customer service, 4 for finance, 5 for a bucket load of patience' (you get the picture) – are efficiency methods that have all compounded a customer 'disconnect'.

For some organizations, the expectation of a customer to be heard, to share their viewpoint and to get challenges sorted out quickly, rather than being a focal point, is a pesky distraction:

- **What?** They've got opinions about our services they think we should listen to?

- **What?** They expect us to answer their queries and keep them updated about a service we are selling them and they are paying for quickly and they get upset when we don't?

- **What?** They want us to admit when we get it wrong, apologize and do something about it?

Reconnecting the disconnect

Realistically, social media connectivity, as technologically advanced as it may at first seem, is actually enabling the very simple reversal of the disconnect between organizations and the people they impact. It is real-time, real-world, one-to-one and one-to-many conversations.

With these social conversations you are not always in control, but when managed, they give you and the organizations you lead the opportunity to genuinely personalize the customer relationship – and by personalization I don't mean simply sending emails saying, 'Hello Michelle'.

Social is taking us back to an era of the local shop mentality, where the business owner would once upon a time make the effort to collaborate with customers – asking them if there was anything else he/she should stock, asking customers what ideas they had for improving services or systems. A perfect example comes from Brian Chesky, the CEO of Airbnb, when on 25 December 2016 he shared a tweet: 'If Airbnb could launch anything in 2017, what would it be?' (Chesky, 2016).

There are some incredible ideas that came from that question, many of which are simple to execute (as you will see in the article referenced at the end of this chapter) and, as an Airbnb host myself, really very highly practical and useful.

We will explore more in Chapter 2 about the 'social audience', who they are, what they look like and more around their expectations, but it's safe to say that technology has empowered all of us as consumers.

Think about the way you yourself now make purchases. Think about the great experiences and also the bad ones.

As markets have become more and more crowded, customer service has become an important differentiator and, thanks to social media, the service delivery bar has been well and truly raised, along with customer expectation.

Of course now, through social networking platforms, not only are we all able to share our views directly to an organization, but at the same time (and sometimes separately), we are able to share our views with anyone else who is willing to listen – our friends, family, strangers, other prospective purchasers – whoever. Customer service has never been so two-way or crowd-way (recall any of those bad service stories that go viral on social?).

Whilst pondering your own service experiences, I want you also to consider whether you have purchased something, or perhaps not purchased something, because of 'shared beliefs'. Are you yourself perhaps a belief-driven buyer?

Belief-driven buyers

Belief-driven buyers are those who switch, avoid or boycott a brand or product based on its stand on societal issues.

The Edelman 2017 Earned Brand Study, 'Beyond No Brand's Land', with 14,000 respondents across 14 countries, measured the strength of the relationship consumers have with brands they buy across 7 dimensions and 18 categories (Edelman, 2017a).

The study identified that shared beliefs are the most powerful driver of commitment to a brand: 57 per cent of consumers are buying or boycotting brands based on the brand's position on a social or political issue; 30 per cent more than identified three years ago.

For belief-driven buyers, silence is not an option: 67 per cent bought a brand for the first time because of its position on a controversial or social issue, and 65 per cent stated they would not buy a brand if it stayed silent on an issue it had an obligation to address. Case in point: in the Appendix you will find that one of the CEOs I interviewed, Dr Sam Collins, provides an example of exactly this relating to Campbell's soup. Whilst she had never really thought about what soup she bought, since their stance against a social media backlash relating to their 'Two Dads' campaign, she is now a forever more Campbell's soup purchaser.

In this ever-increasing connected world, there is a growing responsibility on brands. Belief-driven buyers expect brands to contribute money, time and influence – evident in employee behaviour, day-to-day business activities, sourcing and advertising, with 51 per cent believing that brands can do more than governments to solve ills. Key 'ills' that concern belief-driven buyers are the environment, racial and ethnic divisions, gender equality, economic policy and immigration.

Again, belief-driven buyers are seeking less talk and more action. Where brands actively engage people to act on their belief and drive conversations, this in turn is earning loyalty and new customers.

Sticking with Airbnb, their #weaccept 'Acceptance starts with all of us' campaign started with a 30-second Super Bowl ad in February 2017 (Airbnb, 2017). The campaign initially asked people to sign up to open their homes to house refugees and continues to engage with people daily via social. From a 'social CEO or social leader' perspective, rather than sitting back and letting the marketing and communication teams promote the campaign, to this very day I am writing these words, Brian Chesky is 'leading from the front', showcasing that the objectives of the campaign are a top priority for the business.

A tweet shared by Brian on 26 June 2017 stated: 'Opening the doors to people in need – whether refugees or victims of a disaster – is a top priority for us' (Chesky, 2017).

Why do belief-driven buyers matter to you as a leader?

As the Edelman report summarizes, there is a consumer shift to people buying brands based on their beliefs (Edelman, 2017a). We're seeing more brand campaigns focused on using their influence not only to engage audiences, but to call them to take action.

Brand and its many facets – reputation, management, values – is one of the key responsibilities of the leader (and for leader, read business owner if it is just you!). If 'brand' is out there in the hearts and minds of the customer (and of course, customer can be both internal employees and external consumers), then this provides great opportunity for the 'social' leader to be authentic and transparent in 'living the brand', bringing a human aspect to it and, ultimately, strengthening the all-important consumer–brand relationship.

Where do these belief-driven buyers learn? It is no surprise that they are getting their information from friends, family, press, advertising and, of course, social media.

Jumping back to the 'trust' challenge, what better way of staying in tune with what is going on within an organization than hearing it directly from the CEO or senior representative? The voice of the leader is there to empower, support, educate, update, defend and be held accountable.

It is interesting that Lloyd Blankfein, CEO of Goldman Sachs, whilst he had set up a Twitter in 2011 that had over time accrued over 43 million followers, had famously never tweeted. (He would have fallen nicely into the 92 per cent segment of CEOs who had a social presence – but had never engaged!)

His first tweet on 1 June 2017, which was retweeted 13,000 times and gained over 2,500 comments, was to share his view on the Paris Agreement. To quote his tweet: 'Today's decision is a setback for the environment and for the US's leadership position in the world. #ParisAgreement'.

Since that first tweet in June 2017 he has continued to use Twitter as a communication vehicle. In an interview with CNBC's Jim Cramer about why he has recently started using Twitter, he advised that he is using it to share his opinion on matters from the perspective of being the CEO at Goldman Sachs (CNBC, 2017). Commenting where things fall into their 'wheelhouse of expertise' and on matters that impact his employees, in his own words: 'I've always commented, but before Twitter, I did those things by press release' (Business Insider, 2017).

Beyond broadcast media

When social networks were initially embraced by businesses, the channels were largely the domain of the marketing and communications teams. They were initially seen as broadcast communication channels, to purely share the latest advertising message, promotion or campaign out to the market.

In fact it is still the case that, for a number of short-sighted organizations, social networks are used solely in this perfunctory way: without any focus on the ability to engage, create community, listen and learn.

In reality, beyond the marketing department, many parts of an organization are potentially impacted by social, including:

- R&D – used as a test bed or to watch sentiment of product releases, or to target specific audience for trials, or generally engage in research.
- IT – infrastructures and systems, both internally and externally to support social engagement.
- Customer service – front-line response and engagement, immediate business insights and feedback and service recovery.
- Brand – tracking reputation, reputation management, sharing values, thought leadership.
- Marketing/PR – both internal and external communications; promotions, product launches, advertising, press launches, news to press, brand awareness and brand sentiment analysis.
- HR – recruitment drives, people selection and people monitoring.
- Business development – relationship building, partnership development, key client/partner account monitoring.
- Business insights – competitor analysis, data analysis, market analysis, consumer analysis.

As we move through into Chapters 4 and 5 focusing on strategy and tactics, we will explore how you, as the leader, can use your own social activity to support and align with key initiatives to extend reach and impact.

Seeing around corners

Talking of business insights, when interviewing a number of CEOs and leaders, and from my experience from consulting and training over the years, one key area where social media can really assist is by providing you with the immediate ability to 'tune in' and listen to what is going on in your landscape. As Brian J Dunn put it so eloquently in his interview, 'It allows me to see around corners.'

Admittedly, it is not always the most statistically robust data – but it does give you a temperature check. A key bonus is that it is largely real time, inexpensive and quick, as social media is immediately accessible.

I also interviewed Kevin Burrowes, Head of Clients and Markets at PwC (again, the full interview can be found in the Appendix). Kevin sits on the UK Executive Board with responsibility for clients and markets. He is also the Global Relationship Partner for a global bank. I had initially met Kevin some three years earlier, when invited to talk to Kevin's peers about the adoption of social media within a leadership team.

At that time, there was very little appetite from the leadership team to become involved with social. However, as you will read later, quite a lot has developed over the past three years.

He too mentioned that a key part of social media for him is the immediacy of being able to quickly tune in to what is going on in the landscape. The 'tuning in' is one of the key benefits cited from those I interviewed and is highlighted in Chapter 8.

In fact, all conversations work better when there is a balance between talking and listening and the 'listening' aspect of social media is something that I believe is often underutilized. In Chapter 5 we will cover 'listening' in greater detail – giving you steer as to what you could be listening for, how to cut through unnecessary noise and tune in to what matters for you, and how listening can help you as a social leader.

Leading from the front

Good communications start from within. The better the culture, the more likely it is that social media will succeed. In an ideal scenario, as well as a desire to embrace change, social media goals need to be made clear to everyone in the organization.

Going back to my interview with Kevin Burrowes at PwC, Kevin advised that within PwC there is now formal annual social media training across the business (and yes that is for all 19,000 employees – and it is mandated).

There are even social media exams (yes, I'm going to repeat that… social media exams!) – and the exams are not simply paying lip service to training. Exams need to be passed otherwise the examinee has to keep taking the exams until they pass.

Kevin also advised that within PwC they have created an internal 'social media ranking system', which is effectively an internal league table of active social media team members. The table is published annually so that individuals can assess where they sit and how social they are compared to colleagues, and indeed benchmark their current levels of activity. (When you read Kevin's interview you will notice that his target is to be in the top 10 and currently he is sitting at around the 40 mark!) The embracing of social in this way is in stark contrast to when I met Kevin and a number of his colleagues, just three years ago.

Whilst I was surprised by internal social media exams, it jogged my memory, as I recalled reading an article citing similar activity at Lego (Bold, 2013). Lars Silberbauer, Global Senior Director of Social Media and Video at Lego, was explaining that social media training is encouraged for all senior leadership team members, and not only is it encouraged, but again, there are social media exams.

A few questions to ponder at this point:

- How competent are you and your leadership team in social?
- Have you taken any social media exams?
- Is this a practice in your organization?
- Would you pass?

Sticking with the social media exams theme (relax, take a breath, I'm not planning a test right now), however, I do want to ask you just a few questions before we move on…

First, about your business. Does your business have:

A defined business strategy with key performance indicators (KPIs)?	YES/NO
Focused goals for social media/digital marketing?	YES/NO
A blog/news channel on your website?	YES/NO
A 'growth' mind set – open to new ideas and new trends?	YES/NO
A basic understanding of the benefits of social media and digital communications?	YES/NO
A content plan in place – where to source ideas for relevant and compelling content?	YES/NO
Plans to actively listen to what customers say about your business?	YES/NO
A customer engagement programme in place?	YES/NO

And now over to you. Do you have:

A basic understanding of the benefits of social media and digital communications?	YES/NO
A social media engagement strategy with KPIs?	YES/NO
Focused goals for your social media activity?	YES/NO
A blog/news channel where you share your expertise/views?	YES/NO
A growth mindset – open to new ideas and new trends?	YES/NO
A content plan in place to create relevant and compelling content?	YES/NO
The means to tune in in 'real time' and listen to what your customers say about your business?	YES/NO

My next question…
How do you eat an elephant?
That's right… one chunk at a time.

If you are beginning to feel slightly overwhelmed, take a deep breath and just let it all go. Remember, we are only at the beginning, and trust me, all the juicy 'this is how you do it' is still to come.

My elephant-eating, one chunk at a time mantra, and a model you will become familiar with throughout the rest of this book, is my Smart Social Focus Model (Figure 1.1):

PLAN – LISTEN – ANALYSE – ENGAGE – MEASURE

Figure 1.1   Smart Social Focus Model

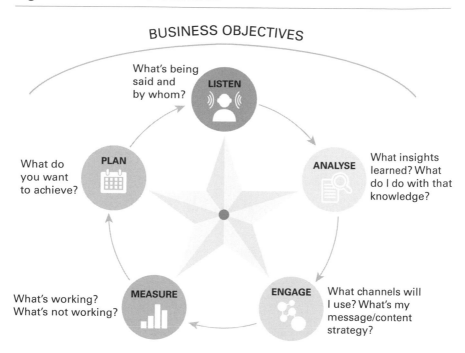

You will note that the dynamics of each element of this model are an iterative process. We will get into this in more detail in Chapter 3, when we explore each aspect of the model, together with your digital footprint and how you currently 'show up' and build your social platform.

For now, we will leave this chapter pretty much where we started, with the importance of the customer.

Focus on the human experience

What I personally found very interesting from the PwC Digital IQ report (PwC, 2017) was largely the recommendations for how leaders realize true potential from digital investments in a rapidly advancing landscape.

Their report states:

The answer is at once simple and infinitely complex: focus on the human experience... This entails rethinking how you define and deliver digital initiatives, considering employee and customer interactions at every step of the way, investing in creating a culture of technology innovation and adoption, and much more. (PwC, 2017)

Remember these three things

1 The pace of change and digital transformation continues at a significant rate and research shows that leaders are struggling to keep up.

2 Social media is one of the social technologies that you can utilize to get closer to the customer to engender trust and engagement. It is an aide to assist you, not hinder you.

3 You are a consumer too. Consider your own experiences and where digital and social fit in.

Take action

As part of your 90-day plan in Chapter 7, we will focus on the 'how to' of each of these key Chapter 1 aspects:

- Write down all the people or organizations you would be interested in tuning in to on a daily basis.

- Ask peers you respect what they think of social media and whether they are active and why.

- Google 'Social CEO' or social and C-suite – and take a look at not only the references I have supplied for you within this chapter, but get a general feel for what is going on with social media and leadership.

References

Airbnb (2017) [accessed 29 November 2017] #weaccept, 5 February [Online] www.Airbnb.co.uk/weaccept

Bold, Ben (2013) [accessed 29 November 2017] Social Brands: Lego Forces Management to Sit Social Media Exams, *Campaign*, 7 February [Online] https://www.campaignlive.co.uk/article/social-brands-lego-forces-management-sit-social-media-exams/1170028?src_site=marketingmagazine

BrandFog (2016) [accessed 29 November 2017] CEOs, Social Media and Brand Reputation Survey [Online] http://brandfog.com/BRANDfog2016CEOSocialMediaSurvey.pdf

Business Insider (2017) [accessed 19 January 2018] Goldman Sachs CEO Lloyd Blankfein Explained Why He Started Antagonizing Trump on Twitter [Online] http://www.businessinsider.sg/lloyd-blankfein-twitter-trump-2017-6

CEO.com (2016) [accessed 29 November 2017] 2016 Social CEO Report [Online] https://web-assets.domo.com/blog/wp-content/uploads/2017/05/Report_SocialCEO_2016.pdf

Chesky, Brian (2016) [accessed 29 November 2017] If Airbnb Could Launch Anything in 2017, What Would It Be?, *Twitter*, 25 December [Online] twitter.com

Chesky, Brian (2017) [accessed 29 November 2017] Opening the Doors to People in Need – Whether Refugees or Victims of a Disaster – is a Top Priority For Us, *Twitter*, 26 June [Online] twitter.com

CNBC (2017) [accessed 19 January 2018] Watch Jim Cramer's Full Interview With Goldman Sachs CEO Lloyd Blankfein [Online] https://www.cnbc.com/video/2017/06/20/watch-jim-cramers-full-interview-with-goldman-sachs-ceo-lloyd-blankfein.html

Edelman (2017a) [accessed 29 November 2017] Edelman Earned Brand 2017 – A Global Survey [Online] http://www.edelman.com/earned-brand/

Edelman (2017b) [accessed 29 November 2017] 2017 Edelman Trust Barometer – Global Report [Online] http://www.edelman.com/global-results

Howes, Scarlet (2017) [accessed 29 November 2017] First Ever Robot Receptionist Gets Job in London and She's Named After Gwyneth Paltrow's Iron Man Character, *Mirror*, 4 July [Online] http://www.mirror.co.uk/news/uk-news/first-ever-robot-receptionist-gets-10738388

PwC (2017) [accessed 29 November 2017] 2017 Global Digital IQ® Survey: 10th anniversary edition [Online] https://www.pwc.com/us/en/advisory-services/digital-iq/assets/pwc-digital-iq-report.pdf

Roberts, K (2016) [accessed 29 November 2017] *64 Shots: Leadership In a Crazy World*, Powerhouse, Brooklyn, NY

Weber Shandwick (2017) [accessed 29 November 2017] Socializing Your CEO IV: The Engagement Factor [Online] http://www.webershandwick.com/uploads/news/files/SocializingYourCEO_FINAL.pdf

02
The social landscape

In Chapter 1, I set the scene around leadership in a social world. Before we set off into the highly practical *this is how you 'get social'* chapters within this book, I feel it is important to provide you with some compelling context around where we are with social today.

Let's call this chapter a 'social landscape scene setter', bringing you up to speed with how social is being embedded within organizations, the rise of mobile technologies, and the impact on changing consumer behaviour. This overview will not only provide you with some interesting facts and stats but will also get you thinking about the wider context and what is coming next.

Regardless of where you or your organization are with social right now, this chapter sets out to show you how social media and other social technologies are being embraced and to provide you with ideas and knowledge to assist you with your own adoption.

What you will learn from this chapter

- Compelling stats and facts around social media adoption (and, because they continuously change, reliable places to source them).
- How technology and mobile technology has enabled social media to be part of our everyday lives.
- The age of the audience: changes in consumer behaviour and expectation.
- Who is on which social media channel and why.

Navigating the social landscape

Since Tim Berners-Lee presented the world wide web to us back in 1990, the world has become far more digitally 'connected'. More than half of the world's population now uses the internet. As of April 2017, according to the 'State of the Internet' report (Kemp, 2017), it is reported that more than 3.8 billion people around the world use the internet, taking global internet penetration to 51 per cent. We have now hit the point where more people in the world use the internet than don't.

Popular social networks – Facebook, Twitter, LinkedIn, YouTube, Google+, Pinterest, Instagram, Snapchat – along with a number of established and growing social messaging sites such as WhatsApp, WeChat and Facebook Messenger are enabling connection and reach beyond the realms of traditional media channels.

At the time of writing, the 'Digital In' analysis report, from We Are Social and Hootsuite (We Are Social, 2017), reports global activity within key social networks around the world as follows:

- Facebook – over 2 billion users
- WhatsApp – 1.2 billion users*
- Facebook Messenger – 1 billion users*
- YouTube – 1 billion users
- WeChat – 889 million users*
- QQ – 868 million users*
- Instagram – 600 million users
- QZone – 595 million users
- Tumblr – 550 million users
- Twitter – 319 million users
- Sina Weibu – 313 million users
- Baidu Tieba – 300 million users
- Skype – 300 million users*
- Snapchat – 300 million users*
- Viber – 260 million users*

- LINE – 220 million users*
- Pinterest – 150 million users
- YY – 122 million users
- LinkedIn – 106 million users
- Telegram – 100 million users*
- Vkontakte – 95 million users
- Kakaotalk – 49 million users*

(*Messenger sites)

The statistics above are indeed significant, and given that Facebook Inc is responsible for Facebook, WhatsApp, Instagram and Facebook Messenger, then Zuckerberg and team Facebook continue to dominate.

But not only do the above statistics illustrate the rate of adoption of these networks in a relatively short space of time, importantly, they also showcase the present number of 'active' accounts. According to the 'Digital In' report, globally there are more than 3 billion people actively using social media (We Are Social, 2017) and the numbers continue to grow. Social media users are *still* increasing at a rate of more than 1 million per day. That is approximately 14 new users every second!

Their report also summarizes that, in all markets and across all the major demographic groups, daily time spent on social continues to rise with each year that passes. According to the Global Web Index Report (Global Web Index, 2017), a survey that has been tracking membership of approximately 50 named social networks/platforms/ apps around the world since 2012, globally, one in every three minutes spent online is devoted to social networking and messaging, with digital consumers engaging with social media platforms for a daily average of over two hours (rising to two hours 40 minutes among 16- to 24-year-olds).

A key driver of social networking, accounting for one-third of our daily internet activity, is the fact that the average internet user now has over twice as many social accounts as they did in 2012. More accounts, more choice, equating to more time spent on social channels.

Of course, by the time you are reading this chapter – the previous stats (and indeed some that follow) will most certainly have changed. However, it is the context of the level of adoption that is the real point I am instilling – so whilst the detail may change, the adoption rate and impact on our day-to-day lives is really what is key.

A world gone mobile

There is no doubt that the pervasion of mobile usage throughout the world is significantly changing the way our human race communicates.

It is safe to say that, globally, we are fast becoming heavily reliant on our mobile phones. A recent study by DScout uncovered that the heaviest smartphone users click, tap or swipe on their phone a shocking 5,427 times a day (DScout, 2016)! Admittedly, that jaw-dropping figure relates to the top 10 per cent of users – however, according to their research, the average number of times the general user touches their phone still came in at a whopping 2,617 times a day!

Regardless of stats, take a look around any street scene, commute, office, restaurant, canteen, park or, infuriatingly, even cinema. It's clear that we are all a little obsessed with our mobile phones and increasingly dependent on being 'connected'.

Undertake a quick search on Google and you will even find an abundance of articles and resources relating to 'mobile phone/smartphone loss anxiety disorder'! Yes, it is a 21st-century genuine disorder. Getting away from it all and 'going off grid' is now a conscious weekend challenge that people gloat about (ironically on social media), rather than the norm.

Making calls via our phones, whilst not obsolete, is generally not the main usage. According to Deloitte's Global Mobile Consumer Study 2016, as of mid-2016, 31 per cent of people don't make any voice calls in a given week (Deloitte, 2016).

Our smartphones offer us a rich suite of apps to help manage our lives and businesses, including personal health, banking, accounting, purchases, productivity, entertainment, connectivity and social networking. In fact, most usage on our mobiles is via mobile apps rather than mobile browsers, so it is perhaps no surprise that 60 per cent of smartphone activity is accounted for by social networking apps. Now, given how reliant we are on our mobiles, 60 per cent being utilized via social media apps is significant. At the time of writing, the total number of unique mobile global users stands at 4.96 billion!

Mobile usage continues to grow, with two-thirds of the entire global population now using a mobile on a regular basis and with smartphones accounting for around 55 per cent of global mobile usage. According to that same Deloitte report, this figure stands at 81 per cent in the UK, a number that has doubled over the past five years.

It is further estimated that around 93 per cent of all internet users now access the internet via mobile devices. With younger generations, or new internet users, having a 'phone first' (or, more likely, 'app first') attitude, that percentage is only set to increase.

Mobile social

Given the above, it is no major surprise to see that mobile social media usage continues to grow at a phenomenal pace. According to both the Global Web Index and the Digital In reports mentioned earlier, mobile social media continues to see the fastest growth across the data points they measure.

Mobile social media users grew by 149 million during the last quarter alone (January 2017 to April 2017), equating to around 50 million new users per month or 1.6 million new users every day. The total number of people around the world accessing social media via mobile devices now stands at just under 2.7 billion, representing a global penetration of 36 per cent. With each quarter that passes, indexes see fewer and fewer people turning to PCs and laptops to access social media.

Remember back in Chapter 1, when I talked about social and mobile technologies totally pervading our lives? These studies and findings provide evidence of just how ingrained the platforms have fast become.

Whilst there are a lot of big numbers to take on board here, the reality is that amongst these huge numbers are your employees, your customers – and your potential future employees and customers.

My question to you as a leader, then, is: if these channels are where your customers and employees are – then shouldn't you be there too?

John Legere, CEO of T-Mobile, who I spoke to, and who seems to have social as well as magenta running through his veins, put it very simply in a tweet published on 19 July 2017:

Of course I'm on social – it's where customers are! (Legere, 2017b)

Now that we have looked at the numbers and appreciate the scale of social networks and of mobile technology as a key driver of social adoption, let's take a look at the impact that social networks and mobile are having on how we communicate.

The changing face of communication

Before we continue to explore how communication has changed, I ask you to pause for a few moments to reflect on the practicalities of your own behaviour.

A few questions to contemplate

- Do you message or text people more often than you call them?
- Do you keep up to date with friends, colleagues or family via WhatsApp, WeChat or other group messenger apps?
- Do you take to your mobile to check on what is happening in the world via your news apps?
- Have you had a conversation recently that has led to either you or a few of you unlocking your phones to check the detail or look something up on Google or any other site?
- What about your service level expectations? Have you realized you needed something and hopped on to Amazon Prime immediately to get it the next day?
- Have you received great or poor service and left an online review? (Or wished you had?)
- Have you checked the reviews on a site such as Amazon or other before you bought something?
- Have you shared an article link, image or video with friends, colleagues, family – relevant to a recent conversation?

If you have answered positively to any of these questions, then you are communicating and consuming in a way that not so long ago just would not have been possible.

Technological advances – the internet, algorithms, mobile, smart-phones and social networks – have shifted how we as human beings both consume things, news and entertainment, and communicate.

These advances have enabled a complete democratization of the way in which we communicate and consume. Armed with just a phone and internet access, anyone in the world now has the opportunity to be a publisher, editor or broadcaster.

The age of the audience

This leads me to the next key point: today, we as consumers (and indeed our clients, customers and audiences) have never been as empowered nor have we had as much choice.

Whether we like it or not, technology has enabled not only an 'always on' society, but also an 'everyone can have their say' society. Consumers have power and everyone has resources at their finger-tips, which enables each and every one of them to be a potential influencer.

A recent report from TurnTo, 'Hearing the Voice of the Consumer' (TurnTo, 2017), highlights:

- 81 per cent of shoppers will pay more and wait longer to receive products that are associated with user-generated content. To be clear, this is content created not by the brand but instead by the now powerful and influential 'consumer'. The content could be a review, a blog post, a tweet, a post on Facebook, Instagram or Snapchat.

- Shoppers under 30 report being more greatly influenced by user-generated content in purchasing decisions than older respondents.

- In the age bracket 18–29, 97 per cent report that user-generated content has an extreme influence.

- Two-thirds (63 per cent) believe that user-generated content provides a more authentic shopping experience.

- 73 per cent state that user-generated content increases their purchasing confidence.
- 61 per cent report that user-generated content encourages them to engage with brands.

Remember that 'trust' issue we discussed in Chapter 1? Well, trust raises its head all along the buying cycle. Consumers are far more likely to trust other consumers than they are to trust marketing messages from brands.

Again, think about your own behaviour. I have lost count of the amount of purchases I have made where I put my total trust in the reviews of complete strangers, over and above the carefully crafted marketing messages and value propositions developed by the brands. From a marketing and advertising perspective, as the leader, involved in understanding what is going to be spent where, what message does the impact of user-generated content, and the power of the consumer, send to you?

To hammer home this point about the power of the ordinary-person influencer in another context, it is useful to reference some of the remarkable political campaigns of recent times. In the United States back in 2008, the Obama campaign highlighted the power of tapping into the ordinary person via social networks. More recently the much-publicized Trump campaign reportedly focused millions of dollars on social media advertising to reach and call to action audiences that ordinarily would not have voted.

Then in the UK, of course, both Brexit and the June 2017 election echoed some of the Trump social media campaign tactics and, in doing so, cultivated 72 per cent more youth voters, amounting to a shock hung parliament. At the same time, content in the mainstream news focused on headlines damning the Labour Party. Once upon a time such news headlines, together with TV debate, may have been the only key influencers.

But that was before the days of social media – days where commentary and opinion shared between individuals galvanized people to hit back against the 'blinding us from the truth' mainstream media, encouraging them to get involved, take a stand and, importantly, take action and vote.

Bringing it back to business, we see the same social media 'influencer/ crowd sourcing' tactics at play. Remember the 'Beach Body Ready' social media backlash (Clarke-Billings, 2015)? Protein World launched its advertising campaign in the summer of 2015. Within a few days, if not a few hours, a backlash against objectification of women had begun. Thousands of people took to social media to call out the brand, pressurizing them to remove the advertisements. The brand firmly took the stance that there was nothing wrong with their ads, defending the campaign. Within a couple of days, a petition had been raised and, thanks to social media, more than 60,000 signatures were received. The Advertising Standards Authority was alerted to the foray and actually banned the ads.

Prior to the campaign, Protein World was not as well known as it was following the campaign, yet this was not necessarily for the right reasons. However, that said, it is reported that sales spiked significantly during the PR circus and social media storm that surrounded the campaign. Like they say, there is no such thing as bad PR! More recently, McDonald's pulled an advertising campaign just four days after an influx of consumer complaints via social media (Rogers, 2017).

But it is not all about backlashes; there are a lot of positive aspects to be gleaned too. The McKinsey Quarterly article, 'The Evolution of Social Technologies', highlights findings from their research of more than 2,700 global executives, spanning the 10-year period 2005 to 2015 (Harrysson, Schoder and Tavakoli, 2016).

It evidences three distinct uses of social media technologies, to paraphrase:

1 **Tryouts**: from the mid-2000s, the testing of social technologies within certain functions such as marketing to acquire new customers and to build interactions with existing customers and influencers.

2 **Collaboration and knowledge work**: starting around 2010, more internal collaborative approach with social, adopting internal social platforms such as Chatter and Yammer (internal Twitter-style platforms) to assist with sharing knowledge, gathering insights and highlighting expertise and talent.

3 **Strategic insights:** more recently social technologies are emerging to be used to support and shape strategy, encouraging internal and external customers to get on board with the crowdsourcing of ideas and innovation. The report cites two case studies – Lego and Daimler – where they are actively engaged in an open strategy initiative. In the case of Daimler's project, some 30,000 registered participants have posted more than 2,000 ideas – and have followed through with successful pilot projects of some of these crowdsourced ideas.

There is no doubt that tapping into the wisdom of the crowd and the ordinary-person influencer can prove beneficial to both leaders and organizations.

Now that we have had a quick look at behaviours on social, let's move on to looking at demographics – and who is on the channels.

A quick look at social channel demographics

Figure 2.1 maps the five generations alive today. Whilst there is debate around where some of the segments start and finish, it is widely acknowledged that there are five separate generations living within the world. Each of them potentially communicates and is perhaps influenced in entirely different ways.

Let's start with Generation Z. Born after 2002, this is the segment of individuals who have grown up knowing nothing other than digital. Their lives are being influenced by technology in ways that have never occurred before. They are the first tribe of true digital natives, sometimes referred to as 'screenagers'.

This 'tribe' believe themselves to be game changers. Thanks to technology, their belief is that there is nothing they cannot do or achieve. They are united in wanting to save and change the world.

There is a very accomplished book, *We Are Generation Z*, by Vivek Pandit who, born at the turn of the millennium, started writing the book at the age of 14 (Pandit, 2015). A regular blogger, with his own website and, naturally, active on the popular social channels, he published the book at age 17 (this alone speaks volumes about this generation and the opportunities that technology enables).

Figure 2.1   The five generations living in the UK

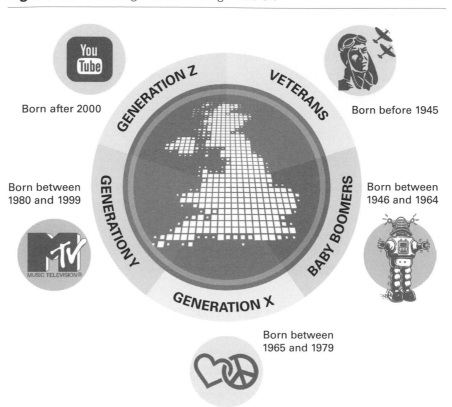

The opening paragraph of his Introduction provides a very telling overview of exactly who this generation is:

I listen to music mainly by streaming it, but occasionally purchase songs online. I have watched movies on DVD but prefer instant downloads. I grew up thinking the war on terror always existed but mainly in the background of my life.

My phones have always had touchscreens. To connect with family and relatives I will occasionally use Facebook, but to communicate with friends I rely on Instagram, Snapchat and Twitter.

For a conversation with one person I prefer texting on my phone, although to contact teachers or relatives I will use email. When researching for homework, I take to the internet. If I need to collaborate with others, I know video hangouts work well. Given the option of constant communication, I like having constant feedback – and I also like to offer feedback through online reviews. I love to shop online, taking time to explore multiple sites and research multiple reviews. (Pandit, 2015)

Amongst this digital tribe are people such as Adora Svitak – a 13-year-old whose TedX talk 'What Adults Can Learn From Kids' to date has 5 million views (TED, 2010).

These digital natives are deemed smarter than the older Generation Y and more conscious of what needs to be done to make the world a better place. Why do Gen Zs matter to you – well, they will be the next generation of employees.

According to a report by agency Sparks & Honey, 60 per cent of Gen Zs want to have an impact on the world, compared with 39 per cent of Gen Y or the slightly older segment, often referred to as millennials (Sparks & Honey, 2014). But perhaps this is down to a youthful and optimistic outlook rather than technological development.

Either way, it is clear that platforms that enable them to share their values and potentially influence others, both locally and around the world, are now readily available to them in their own homes and schools, via the internet, social networks and apps. Putting these Gen Zs into a working environment where these social ways of working don't exist will be like taking a fish out of water.

Remember back to Chapter 1 when we talked about belief-driven buyers – well, Gen Z are belief-driven future employees. They are interested in working for organizations that align with their own beliefs. And where will they be sourcing opinion? Social media.

Moving back along the alphabet we get to Generation Y. Born between 1980 and 2000, this generation is, again, largely shaped by technology. Many a savvy digital millennial has gone on to create some of the world's leading disruptive businesses; think Facebook, Airbnb, Twitter, Uber, Instagram and Snapchat, to name but a few.

Brought up with Google and the internet, mobile phones and text messaging, this segment represents the early adopters of social media and any new technology. Generally speaking, millennials are very digitally savvy and keep pace with the latest digital trends. They have high digital and customer service expectations. Purchasing and receiving goods the same or next day is business as usual, and smart devices and apps are more likely to be a mainstay in both their homes and lives.

Of course, remember that millennials are currently the largest sector of belief-driven buyers. They are also highly likely to be your future C-suite and leadership candidates.

Moving on to Generation X, this is the category I fall into, generally born between 1964 and 1979. From a social network perspective, we are more likely to engage with LinkedIn, Facebook, Twitter and Instagram than Snapchat (but this is changing). The majority of this segment have adapted quickly to new ways of working and have used email for most of their working lives. However, within this segment there are still many who are overwhelmed and long for the days when digital and the 'always on' mindset was not 'business as usual'.

We then move on to the baby boomers. Whole books have been written about the impact of this generation on the world and so I'll keep this section brief. This is the segment born between 1946 and 1964. Even with the emerging disruptive Generation Y and Generation X, most 'leaders', whether Fortune 500 or other, and most political leaders, fall into this age group. Aged between 50 and 70, they fall between those who are comfortable with and welcome new ways of doing business and those who are still grappling with it. From a social network perspective, this segment is more likely to have a presence on LinkedIn (if any), but will not necessarily be actively sharing content.

Last but by no means least, we have the veterans, those born before 1945. Whilst many embrace new technologies, these technologies have not been inherent in their building blocks. Some, of course, will be more digitally in touch than others – and many now make up the ever-growing over-65 demographics on Facebook.

Reading further into the channel demographics, the Sprout Social report (Table 2.1) outlines that 79 per cent of total internet users use Facebook, 32 per cent Instagram, 24 per cent Twitter, 29 per cent LinkedIn, 31 per cent Pinterest and 24 per cent Snapchat. It is firmly placed across the entire customer life cycle. What is clear from the overview of age demographics and the channel usage shown in Table 2.1 is that social and mobile pervades, to greater or lesser degree, all generations.

As I touched on earlier, looking towards the next generation of workers, then clearly a world of digital natives is already starting to

Table 2.1 Social media demographics to inform a better segmentation strategy

Channel	Male	Female	18–29	30–49	50–64	65+
Facebook	75%	83%	88%	84%	72%	62%
Instagram	26%	38%	59%	33%	18%	8%
Twitter	24%	25%	36%	23%	21%	10%
LinkedIn	31%	27%	34%	33%	24%	20%
Pinterest	17%	45%	36%	34%	28%	16%
Snapchat	24%	23%	56%	13%	9%	

SOURCE Sprout Social (2017)

pose interesting challenges for those industries and businesses that are yet to fully embrace current day connectivity.

Today there are more channels than ever before now readily available to organizations to communicate both internally and externally. Therefore, understanding who and where your audiences are enables you to focus on how best to engage with them.

Talking with versus talking at

Historically, brands and organizations would share their marketing messages and campaigns, ideas and views via a number of platforms: TV, billboard, radio and other. As a consumer our choice was to receive it, or ignore it – and if we did indeed want to engage with it then that process was potentially a lengthy one, including writing letters, calling and answering polls etc.

Consumers were not empowered to share opinions to brands and friends and potentially thousands of people by merely typing a short message, sharing a picture or video within seconds, on a mobile device carried around 24/7.

However, jump forward just a few years and whilst traditional advertising channels are of course still relevant, as evidenced previously, they have now merged and integrated with social media channels to assist in directly encouraging the consumer to engage and join in the conversation. No longer do brands and organizations merely talk at their audiences: they talk with them.

If you take a look at the majority of recent cinema ads it is now unusual to find any such productions that miss out on including a social engagement aspect. The intention is clearly to encourage the consumer to get involved with the conversation and expand the reach of the message and continue the digital conversation. No longer are advertisements one-hit wonders, they are continuous conversations. If the advertisement itself does not include the unifying conversational aspect, then it is highly likely that the campaign is being rolled out multi-platform with the social channels having their own tailored 'socially engaging' version of the campaign.

One of my personal favourite ads is the YouTube ad from Samsung (it's the one I never skip). It is part of their #DoWhatYouCant campaign, which showcases an ostrich through his greedy curiosity finding his way into a VR headset and learning to fly (Samsung, 2017). At the time of writing, this YouTube ad has 24,182,881 views on the Samsung official YouTube channel (and no doubt hundreds of thousands more via other channels).

The advertisement description:

> What happens if you refuse to listen to what 'can't be done'? Samsung believes the only way to achieve the impossible is by refusing to accept anything is. #DoWhatYouCant. (Samsung, 2017)

Of course, in line with typical modern-day messaging, this multifaceted campaign covers many media aspects – social media, YouTube ads, cinema ads, billboard etc. A quick search of the #DoWhatYouCant hashtag on Twitter and Instagram (social channels where hashtags tend to be more dominant) will uncover the tens of thousands of conversations from people tuning in via 'social media' and joining the conversation – a simple illustration of talking with rather than talking at and extending the sentiment of the message into the everyday lives of everyday people.

Why does this matter for you as a leader? The Samsung ad demonstrates (as indeed do many others) the 'joined up' approach to using multiple channels to engage audiences in two-way conversations and keep the conversations fluid.

Whilst you may not be featuring in an advertisement, as we will explore further in this chapter, you may indeed be speaking at an event, or even within the organization – and you can keep the conversation going, beyond that event, galvanizing your audience to share feedback, viewpoints and engage.

For you, the key point is moving away from simply pushing out messages, to moving into the continuous conversations space. Skipping back to Chapter 1, it is relevant to repeat the sentiment shared by Brian J Dunn, former CEO of Best Buy, in his interview with me:

> Social media acts as a microphone, allowing you to speak directly to your customers and your employees. When you can respond to consumers directly to help expedite resolution or provide explanation it goes a long way to personalizing the experience. Someone is listening.

Someone is listening...

As the leader of an organization, how powerful that there is evidence that it is you who is listening, that you care about what your customers or indeed employees think, say and do.

Here are a few examples of the tweets I picked up recently when pulling my interview together with John Legere, CEO of T-Mobile. They illustrate a number of points:

> John Legere: Replying to @Andrewvovo @TMobile
>
> 'Congrats on joining the team'. (Legere, 2017a)

> Nate Grey: Replying to @Andrewvovo @TMobile @JohnLegere
>
> 'That day when your CEO likes your tweet'. (Grey, 2017)

> AndrewVovo: Replying to @JohnLegere
>
> 'WOW. Thanks so much for the welcome. Day 2 of training today'. (Vo, 2017)

The above conversation, whilst short, demonstrates the impact of 'listening' and employee engagement. Nice to get a direct welcome from the CEO.

Take a few minutes on John's Twitter channel (or Snapchat, Instagram or Facebook for that matter), and you will see that he is listening in and responding and replying not only to employees, but of course also to customers, competitors and journalists.

From his interview, when I asked questions around the importance of listening, he told me:

> First, I can't emphasize enough the importance of listening. That's still too rare in business. And don't simply listen to what customers are saying about your business. Listen to what people are saying to your competitors. In my industry, I've found that's a great way of learning what not to do. Every leader out there needs to learn and understand the power of social media. These are real people, real customers and prospective customers – and they are giving real feedback that informs our business decisions. Anyone who doesn't see that – is missing a huge opportunity.
>
> Social has changed the rules of the game. It's real-time. It's open and transparent. People want to do business with companies that embrace this. They don't want a suit for a CEO who sits in boardrooms all day. Social can be one of *the* most powerful tools in a CEO's toolbox today – if they'd just be open to it.
>
> The seismic changes we're living through demand that leaders change. I make time for social. And the fact that I can do it from anywhere, anytime on mobile makes it far easier to make time. Having seen the impact of social on my business, I have no intention of slowing down. In today's world, not to put these tools to use would be a dereliction of duty. Social allows us to stay connected to our customers and employees in ways that simply weren't possible before. I'm frankly blown away that more CEOs don't make more time for it.

Social media is part of the job

John Legere, like many other CEOs and leaders, doesn't see 'being social' and engaging with team members, customers, the press and stakeholders as anything other than doing the 'CEO job'. It's a key part of the role. (You can find out more about that in the full interview in the Appendix.)

As Kevin Burrowes from PwC put it:

> I honestly think that business leaders who aren't using social media are missing out. It's a really powerful way to engage with people, both inside and outside of your company, keep up to date with what's going on and also get your own messages across. It's a great way to get your brand across and can really impact how you're seen in the marketplace.

The seamless integration of traditional channels and social channels, and the application of consumers and the general public curating and providing content with organizations and brands, is firmly embedded within the fabric of how we now, in this highly digitally connected age, naturally communicate.

From an expectation perspective, anyone can now tune in to and communicate with anyone, regardless of who they are, be they a world leader, a CEO, a member of royalty or a celebrity. Any barriers to entry are nowadays expected to be well and truly open. The ordinary person is a broadcaster and a potential influencer, with an ever-increasing expectation to be heard.

Such expectation is the impetus behind so many organizations utilizing social media networks as key support and chat channels. Consumers expect real-time lightning-speed responses to tweets or Facebook posts posing questions. Where this is not facilitated, complaints ensue.

What does this mean for you, the leader? Well, we have already witnessed increased levels of 'calling out' of CEOs and leaders by the public on social media. In an article published by Ryan Holmes, CEO of Hootsuite, on LinkedIn's Pulse news network, titled 'Only 10 Per Cent of CEOs Have This Critical Skill', he outlines:

> Big companies have suddenly found themselves in the Twitter crosshairs, from GM and Lockheed Martin to CNN, Macy's and Nordstrom. Leaders are starting to see the power of social media – to connect directly with an audience, respond to crises and put a human face to public announcements. (Holmes, 2017)

If you are out there on the channels, then it is a signal that you are open to conversation. However, if you are not out there on the channels, then you don't have the capacity to join in the conversation directly and respond publicly.

Continuous conversations

Ease of access to connectivity, community and conversation is fast becoming the expected norm – and, of course the conversations, whilst vast in number, are also happening all the time.

In many cases, such continuous conversations are the natural progressive development of discussion following a 'lead event' – be that an actual event, campaign, TV programme, policy, product launch or promotion. Rather than promotional endeavours, campaigns are being positioned as 'conversation openers', thus engaging audiences, current and new, into the one-to-one or one-to-many conversations.

From your perspective, as a leader of an organization, as well as providing you with channels to listen and tune in to the 'word on the street', these channels provide you with the very same 'conversation opener' opportunity too, enabling you to engage with influencers, customers, employees and beyond – whether to seek opinion or to extend the reach and impact of a campaign. Of course, you inspire others to do the same. As a leader you act as a role model within your organization – exhibiting the behaviours you want to see from others.

Straight from the top

In this digital and highly connected age, there is no excuse for not tuning in and listening to customers and, when relevant, being responsive to their comments and questions.

Relevant and potentially insightful conversations are happening all the time, and you and your organization have the opportunity not only to tune in to those conversations to understand the status quo – and potentially learn and develop better systems, processes, products and methodology – but also to lead those conversations and to join in where appropriate. Such engagement presents opportunities for growing audience, share of mind and advocacy as well as having the potential to change perceptions and safeguard reputation.

As evidenced earlier in this chapter, the amount of people now actively engaging on social, the range of demographics and the growing amount of time spent on social channels, and the continuous growth and pace of adoption, present great opportunity for you as a leader of and within your organization to have your say, share your voice, defend your decisions, learn from others, showcase values, and either own conversations or become part of them.

Direct interaction with the customer

Getting closer to the customer and understanding their needs has been a mainstay in many a business strategy for many a year. However, the reality is that few organizations fully execute this in a way that feels authentic, genuine and fulfilling for both the organization and the customer.

Often, the larger the organization, the more hierarchical the layers of management and policy. Getting to a decision and then implementing procedures to open the doors and have direct and transparent conversations with customers (both internally and externally), in reality, regardless of intent, for many organizations is significantly perplexing.

For you as a leader, let's not forget that it can also be just a little bit challenging to put yourself out there. The social activity you engage in most certainly needs to align with your role as a leader – and therefore there has to be clarity of voice, transparency, authenticity and a considerable amount of resilience and safeguarding.

Embracing digital connection requires implementation of processes, people systems, procedure and protocol – all of which enables organizations to engage in and manage genuine and transparent channels of communication. Social networks are just a part of this, but it is an area where you as leader have a great opportunity not just to talk about doing it, but actually to take action.

One of my other favourite mantras is 'activity brings results'. Very simply, it is the getting out there and taking action and 'doing something' that brings about learning and results.

As you will see in the interviews with other leaders in Chapter 8 and the Appendix, their 'social media' practices have evolved – and so will yours as you find your own rhythm.

For you as leader it is about metaphorically stepping out of the office (comfort zone), opening the doors and stepping out into the garden, where the conversations taking place across garden fences exist. You are going to listen, learn, decide what you want to say, get your vocal chords in gear, adapt as necessary and then, ultimately, join in.

Finally, remember, we are eating this elephant one chunk at a time, and these are all aspects we will cover as we develop your strategy and plan of action over the coming chapters.

Remember these three things

1 Social media users are *still* increasing at a rate of more than 1 million per day. This is approximately 14 new users every second!

2 Listening is powerful. Social technologies enable you to tune in, in real time and help you to 'see round corners'. Two ears, one mouth – use them in accordance.

3 The ordinary person is a broadcaster and a potential influencer, with an ever-increasing expectation to be heard.

Take action

As part of your 90-day plan in Chapter 7, we will focus on the 'how to' of each of these key Chapter 2 aspects:

- Become fully conversant with your customer demographics – and include this data as part of management information so that you can analyse trends and keep in tune with where your audiences are likely to be.

- Use the demographic data and customer data to determine which social channels your audiences are using so you are clear on which channels to tune into.

- Leverage the learning from data and insights gleaned from your organization's social media activity. When are your audiences most active, what content engages them, how are they interacting with your social channels? Are there lots of customer service-type questions and, if so, what are key issues that arise? Speak to your social teams and tune in to any insights your social data is revealing.

References

Clarke-Billings, Lucy (2015) [accessed 29 November 2017] 'Are You Beach Body Ready?' Protein World Backlash Grows as Thousands Sign Petition Calling for Removal of 'Body Shaming' Ads, *The Independent*, 26 April [Online] http://www.independent.co.uk/life-style/health-and-families/are-you-beach-body-ready-protein-world-backlash-grows-as-thousands-sign-petition-calling-for-removal-10204601.html

Deloitte (2016) [accessed 29 November 2017] Global Mobile Consumer Survey 2017: The UK Cut [Online] https://www.deloitte.co.uk/mobileuk/#features

DScout (2016) [accessed 29 November 2017] Putting a Finger on Our Phone Obsession [Online] https://blog.dscout.com/mobile-touches

Global Web Index (2017) [accessed 29 November 2017] Quarterly Report – The Latest Trends in Social Networking [Online] https://www.globalwebindex.net

Grey, Nate (2017) [accessed 29 November 2017] That Day When Your CEO Likes Your Tweet, *Twitter*, 18 July [Online] Twitter.com

Harrysson, Martin, Schoder, Detlef and Tavakoli, Asin (2016) [accessed 29 November 2017] The Evolution of Social Technologies, *McKinsey Quarterly*, June 2016 [Online] https://www.mckinsey.com/industries/high-tech/our-insights/the-evolution-of-social-technologies

Holmes, Ryan (2017) [accessed 29 November 2017] Only 10% of CEOs Have This Critical Skill, *LinkedIn* [Online] https://www.linkedin.com/pulse/only-10-ceos-have-critical-skill-ryan-holmes

Kemp, Simon (2017) [accessed 29 November 2017] The State of the Internet in Q2 2017, *LinkedIn*, 18 April [Online] https://www.linkedin.com/pulse/state-internet-q2-2017-simon-kemp

Legere, John (2017a) [accessed 29 November 2017] Congrats on Joining the Team :), *Twitter*, 18 July [Online] Twitter.com

Legere, John (2017b) [accessed 29 November 2017] Of Course I'm On Social – It's Where Customers Are!, *Twitter*, 19 July [Online] Twitter.com

Pandit, V (2015) *We Are Generation Z: How identity, attitudes, and perspectives are shaping our future*, Brown Books, Dallas

Rogers, Charlotte (2017) [accessed 29 November 2017] Are Brands Right to Axe Ads After a Social Media Backlash?, *Marketing Week*, 19 May [Online] https://www.marketingweek.com/2017/05/19/brands-axe-ads-backlash

Samsung (2017) [accessed 29 November 2017] #DoWhatYouCan't Commercial (Online video) [Online] https://www.youtube.com/watch?v=vEEVu4w5LTE

Sparks & Honey (2014) Meet Generation Z: Forget Everything You Learned About Millenials [Online] https://www.slideshare.net/sparksandhoney/generation-z-final-june-17

Sprout Social (2017) [accessed 29 November 2017] Social Media Demographics to Inform a Better Segmentation Strategy [Online] https://sproutsocial.com/insights/new-social-media-demographics/#all

TED (2010) [accessed 29 November 2017] What Adults Can Learn From Kids (Online video) [Online] https://www.ted.com/talks/adora_svitak

TurnTo (2017) [accessed 29 November 2017] Hearing the Voice of the Consumer [Online] http://www2.turntonetworks.com/2017consumerstudy

Vo, Andrew (2017) [accessed 29 November 2017] Woah Thanks So Much for the Welcome! :D :D, *Twitter*, 18 July [Online] Twitter.com

We Are Social (2017) [accessed 29 November 2017] Digital in 2017 Global Overview [Online] https://wearesocial.com/special-reports/digital-in-2017-global-overview

03
The leader's social toolkit

The previous chapters have covered adoption rates and some of the ways social media technologies are impacting the way we now communicate and what that means for you as a leader.

Let's keep front of mind that, whilst social media is a component of digital transformation, in and of itself, the connectivity it enables between people, be they your employees or your customers, is also a key driver of transformation.

For clarity, social media is closely associated with the channels (the tangible tech, the platforms – eg Twitter, Facebook, LinkedIn etc). However, it also represents something you are (engaging, collaborative, connecting and transparent), both as an organization and as an individual.

I certainly don't want to underplay the importance of a robust strategic digital vision that fully integrates social media, both internally across your organization and externally relating to your brand, communications and customer engagement. However, this chapter will focus on how you as an individual and leader can adopt a digital mindset and 'get social'.

Chapter 5 is where we will explore strategic implementation of social media strategy across the business and where your social media activity as leader, or part of a leadership team, fits in as part of that wider digital and social media strategy.

In this chapter I will be starting with where you are right now and how you currently 'show up'. I will be asking you to explore the state of your digital footprint. I will then progress to providing you with a quick and highly practical overview of the leading social media channels, providing a few tips, tactics and context for usage. For LinkedIn and Twitter, two platforms that are more commonly used by leaders for thought leadership, we will take a deeper dive into how to optimize those channels, addressing some of the aspects that many people miss.

I will also touch on other resources that can be helpful, such as scheduling tools and social media management dashboards. Such resources, along with some others, can be particularly useful to help with the all-important 'tuning in', listening and tracking of conversations.

What you will learn from this chapter

- Your digital footprint and why it matters.
- The role social networks can play for you as a leader.
- Useful 'hacks' to optimize your social media activity.
- Tools that can help you to tune in to and track relevant conversations.

I want to start this chapter with a little exercise. It is one that tends to cause a bit of a buzz when I run it as a collective. In fact, it is something you may want to try out with your leadership group or C-suite peers. It is a fairly quick and basic look at just how much 'digital space' you are occupying – and whether what is 'showing up' is as you want it to be.

The exercise is nothing too scientific. I want you to 'google' yourself. Simply open up a web browser and type in your name and assess how you 'show up'. I suggest you also do the same exercise but anonymously via private browsing (incognito), which cleans out browsing history and cookies and allows you to see things as a general user would see them.

Of course, if you're blessed with an unusual name, then for that reason alone it is likely that you will totally dominate the search results. However, the exercise is not a vanity one to judge how dominant your presence is, but rather a simple bit of research enabling you to see from a real-world perspective what is out there about you and, importantly, what is impacting that content. If you are already on social channels, then it's not unusual for those channels to lead the findings.

Your LinkedIn presence is likely to feature in the first few search results. Your LinkedIn profile offers a lot of opportunity for you to optimize relevant content. Of all the social media networks, it is the one network where the content limits are the broadest and for that reason, due to the amount of content and the number of profiles on LinkedIn, the site is heavily indexed by the Google search engines and ranks as highly relevant.

How do you show up?

- What do people find when they search for you?
- How recent are any articles? Are they from years ago – or right up to the current moment?
- Are there any elements that you feel are missing?
- Are you happy with what's out there?

Now do some quick Google searches for some of the social CEOs and leaders highlighted in Chapter 8 and the Appendix. See how they compare.

What you will notice is that for many of them – LinkedIn, Twitter, Google+ and YouTube (and if they are on other channels such as Instagram and Facebook) they feature heavily, usually dominating the top three or four search results.

Given the immediacy and frequency of these social media channels, and given that these leaders are active on their channels, then the content you will pick up is often just a few minutes, hours or, at worst, days old. Effectively, the activity and content being shared on the social channels is assisting with feeding their online presence, so when there is a search presented for them to Google, Google is able to find something current to share.

What could you be doing to influence what's out there?

It may be that if you've got a PR team on board – whether via an internal communications team or externally – then what 'shows up' is already part of a well-planned and well-executed communication strategy.

Even still, the key for you is to look at how you can weave in the social media channels as part of expanding your messages across the various mediums. It is largely impossible to completely control what's out there – whether it's good, bad or ugly. But there are definitely ways you can influence what shows up, in a very timely and simple way via your social media activity.

What could you be doing to influence what's out there?

Alongside any PR and press activity, from a day-to-day perspective you can be influencing what shows up via your social media channels by steering the content you create and curate. (We will cover content in much greater detail in Chapter 4.)

Online visibility covers more than just the social networks, including websites, blogs, advertising platforms and content outlets. Across organizations, these are largely entwined to assist with boosting visibility.

For you personally, it is about getting your digital ducks in a row, creating online 'platforms' to assist your overall presence and message extension. If you look at the associated diagram shown in Figure 3.1 – it is clear that there are a number of ways your online platforms connect with and support each other.

The website could be your corporate organization's site, where you have a presence as either CEO or within the leadership team. Or as is the case with many leaders, you could have your own personal website.

I've shared a few examples here of some really well-put-together personal websites. In each case, they showcase relevant content and clearly link to any relevant social channels: Edward Relf, CEO, Laundrapp: http://www.edwardrelf.com; Lars Silberbauer, Senior

Figure 3.1   Your online platforms and taking an integrated approach

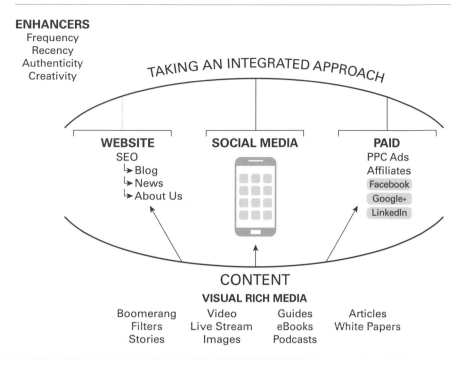

Global Director of Social Media and Video, Lego: http://www.larssilberbauer.com; and Kevin Roberts, former CEO, Saatchi & Saatchi: http://www.saatchikevin.com.

The decision as to whether you branch out and have your own website is really dependent on whether or not it is appropriate. It may also be dependent on whether you as an individual have specific content to fuel it and how your organization's website is structured. The organization's website may already include profiles for key leaders or the CEO, or it may not. If you are a regular voice for or on behalf of the company, whether to the press or as a keynote speaker, then it may be more appropriate to share your 'showreel', or a list of recent talks, speeches or presentations on a personal website, rather than on the organization's website.

Your personal site may include news for the press, your blogs or perhaps details around books you have written or white papers. Effectively, it provides a comprehensive central portal where content, insights and connection can be found. Of course, it can easily be linked to the main website too.

Content plays a critical part of your online visibility. Another key mantra of mine is 'You are what you share' – and the message, statement, video, press release, or perhaps just a simple observation around something topical, is indeed the 'media' – aka the content feeding your online platforms.

Depending on what that content is and what you want to do with it, it can be shared to your own personal blog, or a blog category within your organization's website, for example, 'from the CEO'. It can then be pushed out and shared to your personal LinkedIn profile, either published via the Pulse publishing platform (more on that later) or simply added as a link to your profile. If relevant, your personal LinkedIn content can also be pushed into your organization's company profile and shared in to the news feeds of all employees and anyone following your organization. Such integrated activity keeps employees, stakeholders and the wider community (effectively, anyone who is following and connected to you), fully conversant with your viewpoint, thoughts and activity.

To extend the content even further, you could then create a tweet around the same topic to be shared directly, in real time, including a link to that source content, or via a series of tweets, scheduled in and shared at specific times. Again, depending on the content, message and tactics, other social media channels could be included too and of course the medium of the content may be written word, image, video, live stream or any combination.

From an internal communications perspective, you may have other platforms to consider sharing your messages on too. For example, sharing to the corporate intranet or internal social channels such as Yammer, Chatter or perhaps a bespoke one.

What is evident from the 'your online platforms' diagram in Figure 3.1 is that there are a number of 'outlets' for you to consider how your social presence exists and how you go about influencing it. It may even be that from an organizational perspective you are expected to have a social presence and keep your online platforms well oiled.

As stated in Kevin Burrowes's interview at PwC (see Chapter 8 and the Appendix), not only are team members encouraged to have a social presence internally, but they are also encouraged to use them effectively, with measurement and accountability monitored via an internal 'social ranking table'.

Social media outlets and what they can do for you

Optimizing your online social media profiles is something you can largely control. Before we look at optimization, let's first look at the most common social media networks and what they can provide to you in a leadership context.

From a leadership perspective, it is likely that you are either already plugged in to LinkedIn in some way and perhaps even Twitter too. As identified in the studies in Chapter 1 (and evidenced in the real-world cases in the Appendix), those two networks are currently, by far, the two key networks used by leaders – but certainly not exclusively.

Therefore, it is useful to provide you with a quick overview of the other networks too, as they are most certainly not to be discounted. As we will look at in Chapter 5 when we focus on strategy and tactics, like any other endeavour it is all about having the right tools for the job. In the social media landscape it is about context and showing up where your audiences are.

It may be that there is a case for you personally to create a presence on Facebook or Instagram – or even Snapchat. If your audiences are highly active on those channels and you want to speak to and engage with them directly, as is the case for example with T-Mobile's CEO, John Legere (again, see full interview in the Appendix), then those channels can prove highly significant.

Going from doing no or very little social media activity to suddenly positioning yourself as 'social leader' extraordinaire is not the right way to approach it. In fact, one of the key takeaways coming out of the interviews with other leaders (Chapter 8 and the Appendix) is to start with one or two channels, get them working really well for you and then perhaps consider expanding. After all, you've already got your hands full leading and driving a business or team.

Considering the Smart Social Focus Model outlined in Figure 3.2, before you go anywhere near the 'engage' aspect and rather than diving straight in, it is wise to get your house in order so that you are clear on the why, what, when and how and determining which channels make the most sense for you. Of course, testing and measuring is also essential and we will look at this further in Chapter 6.

Figure 3.2   Smart Social Focus Model – organization

From my experience of working with senior leaders, Twitter and LinkedIn are two of the key channels to start making headway with. Whilst they are the two channels that naturally lend themselves to fitting in with the communication role of a leader, as stated earlier, dependent upon what you are looking to achieve, it may be that other channels are part of your social platform mix too.

Twitter

Twitter in 20 seconds

Twitter is a useful platform for communicating, researching, brand building, marketing, initiating connections, networking and conversation. Messages are now limited to 280 characters.

Topline uses for leaders

- Twitter enables you to quickly keep your eye on the ball in areas you're interested in. The brevity of the messaging means you can quickly skim through your feed and pick up the general gist of what is happening. There is always the option to explore further if you wish to.

- Twitter allows you to check out what influencers, companies, competitors, world leaders, markets and customers are communicating. It also enables you to see any associated conversation and hashtag threads, thus discovering potential new influencers or thought leaders, opinions and joining in conversations, commenting and sharing your viewpoint.

- Twitter is a broadcast channel. You can share company updates, news and press releases, product launches and event info, but it should not be used solely for this purpose. The art of Twitter is to engender engagement, conversation and connection. Used purely as a broadcast channel, your profile can start to look like a stream of promotional one-way spam.

- As part of its broadcasting qualities, in a similar way to Instagram Live, Facebook Live and Snapchat Live streaming, Twitter has its own 'live video' streaming application, powered by Periscope. Once upon a time, live streaming on Twitter was via the Periscope app, but Twitter has now built the live streaming facility, powered by Periscope, into their native app. When you 'go live' on Twitter, your followers will get your live stream tweet in their feeds and they can engage by commenting or sharing emojis across the screen.

Twitter is also an alternative and potentially more accessible channel for people to make contact with you and for you to make contact with them. As stated previously, most of the CEOs and leaders I interviewed for this book, I made contact with via Twitter. If you are on Twitter, it's a signal that you're open for conversation.

LinkedIn

LinkedIn in 20 seconds

LinkedIn is the network people come to for business. It is the ultimate collection of online business professionals and organizations, enabling members to manage current connections and facilitate new ones.

Topline uses for leaders

- LinkedIn is your professional online presence. As a business professional it is expected that you have a well-executed, up-to-date LinkedIn profile. As a leader, it provides you with the opportunity to showcase your personal brand, skills, expertise, experience and credibility. Content within the profile includes opportunity to share rich media, videos, slideshare or presentations. It is an ideal hub for showcasing the latest talking-head videos, press releases, corporate updates, statements, thought leadership articles and white papers etc.

- LinkedIn is also a useful networking resource. It not only enables you to keep in touch and manage all your contacts in one place, it also acts as a dynamic contact management system, keeping you alerted to any role changes, articles, updates or news that your connections share.

- LinkedIn also allows you to develop new connections. It is a way for people to make contact with you, either directly or through a shared connection.

LinkedIn Pulse

LinkedIn Pulse in 20 seconds

LinkedIn Pulse is the tailored news feed covering topical stories from influencer news sources and the Pulse publishing platform from LinkedIn. It includes the latest industry-specific news, news from colleagues and news trending at relevant companies.

Topline uses for leaders

- LinkedIn Pulse offers a tailored news feed. It is a useful resource for you to tune in to tailored news and articles. Pulse also provides a useful publishing platform for your own thought leadership pieces, articles or blogs. Publishing to Pulse is effectively like running a blog via LinkedIn. The articles you publish are automatically pushed into your profile and news feed so that others can engage. Articles are retained on the Pulse network to be searched for and randomly found by others. They can also be selected for a 'spotlight' feature, which provides an opportunity to significantly increase your reach.

Facebook

Facebook in 20 seconds

Facebook is the world's largest social network. Since starting off as a means for keeping in touch with friends and family – sharing updates, photos and videos – the platform continues to evolve. Facebook Groups enable the development of open and closed communities. Facebook is fast becoming the largest advertising medium in the world, offering unparalleled granular audience targeting.

Topline uses for leaders

- Public figure 'Page'. The use of Facebook from a 'leadership' perspective will largely come down to the type of business you are leading and what is relevant for you. It may be that you already have a Facebook profile that you use to keep in touch with your family and friends. Depending on the business, your role and your leadership style, it may or may not be relevant for you to integrate your work and personal lives. To enable you to have a public profile from a corporate perspective, but as yourself rather than the corporate Facebook profile (and enabling you to keep any personal profiles totally separate), a good use of Facebook is to set up your own business profile as a public figure. This will enable you with all the benefits of having visibility, messaging and connectivity via Facebook, but you will be keeping your personal profile well and truly private.

- Groups. A group is a community of people and friends who support one another online. Groups can be 'open', meaning anyone can see the group members as well as the posts; 'closed', where people can see group members but not the posts; or 'secret', where both members and posts are hidden to non-members. From a leadership perspective, it may be that you want to set up a group for, say, market research – inviting specific influential, active key customers to participate in product testing, market research, beta product launches etc. It is more likely to be something your organization does rather than you personally, but as cited earlier, that is dependent on your organization and you. If you are looking to grow thought leadership, then running Q&As and sharing articles into a selected group can be beneficial in assisting you in growing that awareness and reach.

- Facebook Live broadcasting. Whether you have decided to have your own profile, or simply tune into the corporate one, a key area to know about as a leader is the Facebook Live feature. Effectively, it is live broadcasting to your page, community or group. In just the same way as if you were being recorded for a press release, you can also stream the recording live to Facebook. If it is a message that is relevant to the organization's Facebook page, you can share it with those who follow your page. The minute the live starts, followers will be notified that the live is happening. Of course, planned lives get even more engagement. Ensuring your audience knows that the CEO or leader is going live at a specific time (perhaps even as a regular feature), gives opportunity for more of the audience to join the conversation.

Instagram

Instagram in 20 seconds

Instagram is a simple and fast way to share your life with those who follow you via photos and short videos via your mobile.

Topline uses for leaders

- You can share your day via Instagram Stories. Instagram Stories is perfect for a product launch or 'behind the scenes' insights. It gives you the ability to share creative updates like pictures and videos in real time with your audience. Instagram Stories last for 24 hours and they can include as many posts as you like. If you don't want posts within your story to disappear you can save them as posts to your Instagram feed.

- A number of CEOs are turning to Instagram Stories to showcase their day-to-day activity. Take a look at Spencer Rascoff, CEO of Zillow Group, who regularly creates Stories on his Instagram account. As does John Legere, CEO of T-Mobile. Whilst it's about you running your own race, it's always useful to see how others are using this feature on the platform.

- Instagram also allows brand building. You can share an Instagram post a day, relating to something you are doing or your viewpoint on what your organization is up to. Again, John Legere, CEO of T-Mobile, and Spencer Rascoff, CEO, Zillow, for example, both share an image or video a day, keeping audiences in touch with either personal business or campaign activity. It may be as simple as you reposting what your organization is up to and aligning with relevant and popular hashtags.

Snapchat

Snapchat in 20 seconds

Snapchat is a mobile app messenger service that allows people to express themselves via sharing pictures and videos in the moment.

Topline uses for leaders

- A picture speaks a thousand words. Taking a 'Snap' and adding annotations, filters, doodles, location, temperature, date, time, altitude, speed (yes there are a few automated options!) can provide a quick and creative way to share a marketing message, a behind-the-scenes or an interesting way of communicating via group chats internally within teams. Snaps are designed to disappear after 10 seconds. Snapchat pioneered the 24-hour 'Stories' feature (which works as explained above in Instagram), and a 'Memories' feature means that stories can now live on longer than the 24 hours (similar to a camera roll on your phone).

- Brand building. Snapchat currently leads the way with augmented reality filters, with other networks following suit to catch up. It can be useful to share a 'snap' a day or add to a Snapchat story to align with organizational messaging.

Google+

Google+ in 20 seconds

Less of a social network and more of a social and content dashboard, G+ is intended to pull together all of Google's peripheral products (Gmail, Maps, search, Calendar, Hangouts).

Topline uses for leaders

- Google+ is particularly helpful for its Google search engine exposure. If you're using Google apps, then by default you will have a G+ profile. My advice is that to assist with online visibility you optimize it and include links to your other social and online presences so that when your profile comes up in search, people can see the other channels you're on.

- Research. G+ communities can be useful to tune in to see what's out there. However, the challenge is that there are hundreds of thousands of communities. In my experience, G+ communities are time intensive to search and find the relevant ones. Similarly, running your own community is possible, but again, don't underestimate the time required. In my view, whilst having a presence on G+ is important, regularly posting and engaging in communities is not something that I recommend as part of an individual's social strategy. Yes, have a profile, yes optimize it. But let the organization focus on any brand building, community building.

WhatsApp

WhatsApp in 20 seconds

WhatsApp is a mobile messenger app facilitating one-to-one or group messaging and content sharing.

Topline uses for leaders

- Team messaging. WhatsApp groups provide simple and effective messaging systems within teams, both remotely and internally. Beyond internal 'bespoke' messaging systems that may pose certain constraints on teams, using an app such as WhatsApp (which people are already often familiar with) provides a friction-free, simpler and often more productive way to work. It is highly likely that you are already engaged with WhatsApp, and it can be a really useful resource for group messaging with key teams. In fact, at the time of editing this chapter, it was announced that WhatsApp is launching a business-specific version.

YouTube

YouTube in 20 seconds

YouTube is currently the largest free video-sharing service in the world, where users can create a profile, upload videos, and watch, like and comment on other videos.

Topline uses for leaders

- Brand building/playlist. If your organization already has a YouTube channel, you can create a 'leadership' playlist for all relevant videos. The playlist can be shared internally and, if relevant, be open for anyone to view on YouTube.
- Thought leadership. Just as with Facebook Live or Twitter's live streaming, you can live stream to YouTube. In fact, there are apps

that enable you to live stream to all channels at the same time. Even if you are not live streaming to YouTube, you can upload videos created directly to your playlist on the channel. For example, at the time of writing, T-Mobile's channel has around 149,000 subscribers and 18 playlists. 'From John, the CEO' is a playlist that they feed all his live videos and promo videos to and it includes anything that focuses on what the CEO is doing.

Social media channel 'tips'

In my previous book, *The Business of Being Social: A practical guide to harnessing the power of Facebook, Twitter, LinkedIn and YouTube for all businesses,* we broke down each social media channel and provided a detailed and guided step-by-step walk-through of how to set up each channel and optimize it (Carvill and Taylor, 2015). In this book, I'm not going to replicate those instructions. The focus of this book is rather on strategy and tactics, providing you with shortcuts and insights that cut through the masses of advice out there and give you practical direction. It is meant to steer you in your social media strategy and tactics, rather than set-up.

Even though some of the technical aspects of the channels may have changed a little since 2015, that book will still provide you with a highly practical 'how to' resource. You will also find some useful 'how to' set-up instructions over on the blog of this book's online resource site – www.getsocial.site.

Here, what I believe will be more helpful for you to consider are some useful pointers to help optimize your activity, as set out below.

Keep your username simple

Unless it fits with your positioning, there is no need to get overly clever with your profile username.

If you are using social media for business and as part of your leadership outreach, then you really want people to search and find you easily and for them to quickly know it is your account. You will note that a lot of leaders and CEOs simply stick to using their name and this is for good reason.

Endeavour to keep it simple, and where possible secure your name as your profile name – eg @michellecarvill. Where you cannot do that because it has already been taken, perhaps include an initial, eg @michellejcarvill. Even then the search term Michelle Carvill would still bring up my profile in the social search results.

Be consistent with your profile image

You want a decent headshot that you are proud of and that show-cases you.

From a leadership perspective, my advice is to stick with the same picture wherever you position yourself online. On most of the channels you also get a background image too – so again, aim for consistency. Your Twitter, Facebook, Instagram, G+, LinkedIn and YouTube accounts should ideally all look and feel the same. You don't want 'multi' brands out there. You want that simple, identifiable image that shows up across all your channels, making you instantly recognizable.

Visuals matter

Visual content plays a huge part in grabbing attention and encouraging people to engage. Each of the social channels has evolved to fully support and, in some cases, assist in generating visual content (for example, live streaming and apps).

Do a quick Google search and you will find hundreds of references to research showing that posts with images or video significantly outperform pure text. I would suggest that 90 per cent of your posts include engaging visual content.

Get verified

In line with people finding you easily and recognizing it is you, getting verified not only assists with people knowing they are on the right profile, but it adds the trust factor. Getting verified is not a vanity thing, it's a trust thing. The verification badges are not managed by bots. The verification process is managed by teams within the networks who assess each request. The little blue verification badge is therefore highly coveted. Each channel has their own specific process for getting verified, so it is a case of making the request, providing as much relevant information as required, showcasing your reasons (for example if you've got a common name, so as not to be confused with others etc) and then waiting. This applies to Twitter, Instagram and Facebook.

Tag along

On Instagram and Facebook, when you share an image you can include @tags in either the description text, or on the image. On Twitter when you share an image (another good reason for including images in your tweets) you can tag up to 10 people. Of course, they don't have to be 'in' the image to be tagged. It's just a neat way of alerting them to the content as they will receive a notification that they have been tagged.

Pin a tweet or post

On Twitter, Facebook and Instagram you have the option to pin a tweet or post so that it stays at the top of your timeline. I suggest that if there is something pertinent that you want everyone to see when they find you, then pin that. It could be a tweet or post aligned with a campaign, a key personal brand message, or a message linking through to a cause you are supporting or a thought leadership piece. You can, of course, change your pinned tweet or post at any time.

Let's now take a look at some specific tips relating to specific platforms.

Twitter tips

For a Twitter post, 70–101 characters (used to) perform best.

The maximum number of characters for a tweet has historically been 140. However, research showcases that the tweets that get the most engagement are generally shorter, around 70–101 characters. Short and punchy goes down well on Twitter, particularly if accompanied with a relevant image and/or a link to click through to.

At the time of writing, Twitter announced their expansion to 280 characters – effectively doubling the message capacity. However, they do not expect user tweets to change that dramatically. Following tests in September 2017, they found that only 5 per cent of tweets sent were longer than 140 characters and only 2 per cent were over 190 characters – still 90 characters short of the new limit.

It is too soon to advise you on whether short form or long form plays out best, as the function is still too new. My advice is to test it yourself and see what gets the best engagement.

Profile bio

Keep it short and punchy. On Twitter you have 160 characters for your profile biography, but that doesn't mean you have to use them all. Be concise and aim to add a little personality too. If you are going to use a #hashtag, ensure it makes sense. If relevant, don't forget to link to your organization's @tag to include a direct link to that Twitter profile. Apart from the word count there are really no restrictions. If you want to share information around your interests, things you've done to personalize it, you can.

Some examples:

My bio states: Founder @CarvillCreative | Digital marketing & social media pro | Author #GetSocial #BusinessofBeingSocial #social-CEO #yogakeepsmesane (Carvill, 2009)

Ryan Holmes, CEO of Hootsuite, states: Entrepreneur, investor, future enthusiast, inventor, hacker. Lover of dogs, owls and outdoor pursuits. Founder and CEO of Hootsuite. Support? @hootsuite_help (Holmes, 2007)

Lloyd Blankfein, CEO of Goldman Sachs, currently states: CEO @GoldmanSachs (Blankfein, 2011)

Repurpose and reposition – don't rely on the one-hit wonder

Unlike other networks, Twitter operates a 'real time' stream (unlike Facebook, there aren't any algorithms deciding who sees what), so all tweets that are shared, if you are tuning in to them (following them), will show up on your timeline. In short, if you send 10 tweets and I'm following you, your 10 tweets will show on my feed so I can see what you are tweeting about.

What this means is that the more people you follow, the busier the feed. Hence tweets often get missed and therefore, if it is an important message, it's good practice to reposition the message in different ways over a period of time to ensure the message has more chance of getting out there. (More on message scheduling in Chapter 7.)

Thread together

When people or organizations want to say something longer than the original 140 characters without taking people away from Twitter, they simply 'thread' the content. Threads have always existed but there has been a big spike in popularity in 2017. Twitter threads focus on getting engagement. From conspiracy theories, political rants, campaign discussions, ghost stories – the thread story can be anything. Starting a thread is simple – the initial tweet leads and then you simply continue to reply to your own tweet (removing your @tag at the beginning) with the insertion.

Of course, going back to the new extended 280-character tweet, this is likely to have an impact on the tactic of threading tweets together. It may eradicate the need to thread entirely. Or it may create more of an opportunity to create a longer-form story. At this stage, it is too soon to say.

Hashtags: don't overdo them (Twitter isn't Instagram!)

What is a hashtag and how do they work are questions I still get asked quite a lot. Whilst hashtags have become ubiquitous in our online activity, and have even become part of everyday language, many are unsure about how to apply them. From a practical perspective, it is a way of linking or directing people to a topic, a simple seek-and-search function. For example, Coca-Cola's billboard advertising may state #ShareaCoke. Social channels will aggregate all posts that include #ShareaCoke. (You will note that Google search will showcase such findings too.) Using hashtags in your messages enables your content to form part of that story. It is a simple way of jumping into a topic or stream of conversation. My advice is to stick to one hashtag per tweet and a maximum of two. Otherwise, your message is in danger of looking spammy and off point.

Tuning in

If you're not sure about getting started with Twitter and you're not keen on actually tweeting then you could join the millions of people (around 45 per cent) who use the network as a targeted news feed. Tuning in to people, celebrities, thought leaders, influencers, brands, news outlets, sports updates, helplines, travel updates, even competitors – is very accessible via Twitter. As of course is tuning in to your own organization or hashtags around relevant conversations so that you can pick up the general gist of how things are going.

If you follow someone, you are 'tuning in'. If you want to tune in without people knowing you are tuning in, a simple way to tune in privately is to create a private Twitter list. Add relevant people or organizations to that list and then see the tweets in that list (or indeed pull that list through into a social media dashboard).

As is revealed by a number of those I interviewed in Chapter 8 and the Appendix, the immediacy of being able to see what people are saying and how they are reacting is something that many find useful.

Instagram tips

Hashtags – go to town!

On this highly visual mobile app, the main aspect you see is the image or video. The message content is relatively secondary. For Instagram posts it is all about the visual. Interesting, authentic, wow imagery is great – and using your content to tell stories is even better. But it's the hashtags you use to accompany the content that will assist in getting your content out there.

Hashtags provide not only the opportunity to extend the reach of the post but also assist with the context of the visual. You can include up to 30 hashtags on a post – and many people do. In fact, to reinvigorate a post or to extend the reach even further, people also include hashtags in the first comment too.

Find the hashtags that are relevant and popular

Check out Hashtagify.me, which is a tool that helps you to identify key hashtags on certain topics and it is always useful to use some widely trending hashtags, where relevant, such as #instagood #instadaily #instagreat #nofilter (providing you are not using one of their filters).

Like with many things in life, it is about finding a balance. Find a balance of wide-reaching popular hashtags and niche hashtags and, of course, you can create your own set of hashtags, aligned with your organization, brand or personal brand. 10/10/10 is a good ratio.

Tip within a tip If you create a set of hashtags that you are going to use consistently, copy them to the notes function of your phone so you can easily copy and paste groups of hashtags in to each post. This saves you time in typing each one individually – and brings consistency.

LinkedIn tips

Get to All Star

Ensure that you have completed everything you need to on your profile and that when you are in the editing mode, your profile status is 'All Star'. Not only does this improve the chances of your profile being found – as LinkedIn's algorithm favours All Stars above those who have set up a profile but haven't done anything with it (enabling you to be more visible in searches) – but importantly, it just looks more professional and credible.

I often get asked the question as to why, when everything has been completed on a profile, it still doesn't show as 'All Star' status. The main culprit tends to be that whilst people have included job titles, they haven't included a short description. So that is one aspect to check.

Check out your Social Sales Index (SSI)

Aligned with LinkedIn's Sales Navigator resource for sales professionals, whilst you may not be as interested in the 'sales' aspect directly, the index is quite a useful resource for benchmarking your personal brand and relationship activity. Visit https://www.linkedin.com/sales/ssi to view your dashboard and see how you compare with others in your sector and network.

Think personal website and not CV

As with your bio on the other social networks – you want your profile headline to be punchy and to the point. Perhaps because of LinkedIn's heritage, many still complete their LinkedIn profile as if it is purely a CV resource rather than a well-optimized professional online microsite.

For example, in the professional services world, a number of profiles of a leadership team I was working with simply stated 'Partner' in their header. That doesn't really give a lot of context to understanding specialisms or key focus. Your header gives you the chance not only to give your position but also to showcase the impact you make and add a bit of personality. Since the LinkedIn platform revamp in late 2016, only the first two lines of your profile now show in searches, so it is wise to keep your most impactful content up front and centre.

Format it your way

Whilst LinkedIn enables you to enrich your profile by adding visual media – videos, presentations, images and graphics to each section – there is not a basic text-formatting tool.

If you want to add bullet points or embolden things to make reading your profile online more digestible and easier on the eye than large blocks of bulky text (which can be very difficult to read online), then I suggest you create the content in a word-processing system such as Word, in the format you require, and then copy and paste it into LinkedIn.

Due to formatting limitations not all formatting will be retained, but if you have been wondering how some people are able to edit their profile in more reader-friendly ways, well, now you know.

Turn off updates when editing

If you are doing some general housekeeping of your profile to better optimize it, it is wise to turn off the 'sharing profile edits' in the privacy-setting section. Generally, there is a lot of granular functionality in the settings area of all the social networks, so it is wise to familiarize yourself with what is available.

Personalize your public URL

When you create a LinkedIn profile, you automatically create a 'public' profile. The public profile is visible to people when they are outside the LinkedIn platform. You can determine what is on your public profile via the settings function (see top right-hand corner when you go in to edit your profile). You have the opportunity to personalize the public URL. This is fairly simple to do, but many don't do it. If you haven't personalized it, you will see a long string of characters.

My personal URL is www.linkedin.com/in/michellecarvill. It is a much cleaner way of sharing that profile URL and, generally, it just looks a whole lot more professional on your profile.

Connect with context

If you want to make a connection, then best to do it via your desktop rather than your phone.

Your desktop version of LinkedIn allows you to personalize the message when asking someone to connect. If you connect via your phone, the standard robotic 'I'd like to add you to my professional network' message is automatically sent and, personally – and I know this is the case for a lot of people – those automated messages just get totally ignored. If you want to connect, then take to the desktop and add some context and reasoning behind it.

Those are just a few of the tips. As already mentioned, you will find practical hand holding on each of the channels in my previous book, and I'll continue to share more useful tips as things arise via the www.getsocial.site. There are a number of really useful apps you can tap into too, which assist with a range of activity – from finding out who is influential in your feeds to useful management and scheduling tools. I have created a list of some of the ones I find the most useful – and again, you'll find them over on the www.getsocial.site.

To dashboard or not to dashboard – that is the question

Another question I get asked a lot is what is the best way of managing the multiple accounts.

We will look at this in more detail in Chapter 7 when we pull your activity plan together. However, one aspect to consider is whether you choose to centralize your activity via a social media dashboard.

Social media dashboards, and there are now many to choose from, came about to assist people with multiple social media accounts to manage their activity. In the early days of social media, the networks didn't have their own native means of scheduling posts. It was a case of post it and go. As adoption grew, so did the array of social media scheduling tools.

Which social media channels you choose to be active on will influence whether or not you venture into using a dashboard. Dashboards are largely used by agencies and organizations. As an individual, from a 'posting' and engaging perspective, you may find it simpler to engage directly with the native channels.

The most popular social dashboards all have an app version and are readily available via your smartphone. You can feed in multiple channels with the intention that if you create one message, you can select which channels to push it out to.

Of course, the challenge with dashboards is that each social media channel behaves differently. We have already touched on the different use of hashtags on Twitter and Instagram, so there are functional differences to consider. There are also differing character restrictions and, importantly, different audiences. Audience and indeed tone of voice may differ from channel to channel. For example, on Instagram your positioning may be slightly different in tone to, say, your LinkedIn audience.

That said, dashboards can be really useful for helping you to schedule your activity, enabling you to plan ahead and align messages with organizational campaigns, or events. Another good feature of dashboards is the 'listening' aspect, the ability to tune in to streams of conversations, all in one place. Depending on which dashboard you choose, there are ways you can stream specific hashtags, keywords, accounts or even Twitter lists into your dashboard, so that you can view what is happening around those aspects from a centralized perspective.

Dashboards I personally find really useful, and which are hugely popular, are Hootsuite, Buffer and Sprout Social. Each of these has enterprise solutions but, as stated, depending on what you are doing, if just a handful of accounts, they offer free versions that can be useful from a personal user perspective too.

Of course, over the years, some of the channels themselves have evolved to offer scheduling. Facebook offers scheduling options. In fact, if Facebook is a channel of choice, I would highly recommend using that platform natively rather than with third-party apps feeding content to it. It's a better experience all round for yourself and the way the content shows in the channel. For example, when using dashboards, there are sometimes restrictions on how images are displayed. There is also reference to the fact that you made the post via a dashboard, which directly tells people that you are likely to be scheduling content in advance, rather than being spontaneous. This is not necessarily a bad thing, but there may be times where you want things to appear a bit more spontaneous. When you are live on the native platform, you are able to see what is trending in real time, which may also provide you with some creative stimuli.

Twitter also has a lesser-known scheduling option. It is less popular as you have to have set up an advertising account (but not necessarily be using it) to use the scheduling resource; see https://ads.twitter.com. And at the time of writing Instagram has just introduced a native scheduling tool.

Your digital brand

As a CEO, leader or aspiring CEO, there is more opportunity now than ever before to showcase your personal brand, influence your internal team, peers, networks and audiences, both internally and externally.

Social engagement, and being bold and sharing your authentic voice, expertise and opinion via these far-reaching communication channels can have significant impact. As a CEO or senior leader, you hold the position as chief storyteller for your organization, the voice of the company. Highly accessible by the many, digital platforms enable you not only to amplify the reach of that voice and share lessons and values, but importantly to engage with others, to listen, to tune in, to converse, to support, to encourage, to motivate and to inspire.

This has always been the role of the CEO and senior leader internally. However, as we explored in Chapters 1 and 2, technology is changing expectation and there is a growing movement of CEOs and leaders sharing these aspects to the outside world, to assist with humanizing the brand or business. Regardless of B2B or B2C, think

P2P: people to people. People do business with people. Going back to the research cited in the Edelman Trust Barometer Annual Global Study, 2016 and The BrandFog 2016 study (Chapter 1):

- Two out of three people say their perception of a CEO impacts their opinion on the company.
- Having a senior leader show openness provides feelings of accessibility.
- Four out of five employees would rather work for a social CEO/leader.
- 81 per cent of people believe leaders who are active on social media are better equipped to run a company.

In fact, a recent article on Bloomberg Technology illustrates this point very well, citing the case of CEO of Banco BTG Pactual, Roberto Sallouti, following in the footsteps of Lloyd Blankfein of Goldman Sachs, and taking to social media to build transparency and trust. In the article Roberto Sallouti states:

> We had this reputation of being a secretive, closed institution and we wanted to change that, to be seen as transparent, communicative. And the way to do that was through social media – to our surprise, it's been working really well. (Marques, 2017)

Your digital mindset

Of course, it is not just about 'getting social' and building your digital brand, but rather it is about adopting a digital mindset and embracing change and the fact that digital channels, including social media, are very much part of the consumer journey. For those still sceptical, there is no escaping that the expectation of your audiences, both internally and externally, has and will continue to change.

As Caron Bradshaw, CEO of Charity Finance Group (CFG), puts it so finely in her interview:

> To me the growing importance of CEOs and leaders being transparent and authentic, and the changing pace of business, both mean that failure to engage with social may leave you behind. The generation of workers

we are increasingly employing and engaging with were brought up with social media as an integral part of their networking and communications – Snapchatting, WhatsApping and other 'ings' that I don't personally currently use that actively. It feels rather luddite to refuse to engage – a bit like sticking to fax when email came in!

Stop calling it social media

Before we move on to Chapter 4 and focus on 'Content', we should recognize that, for many, the issue with social media isn't everything it enables, but rather that there is a bit of 'fixed thinking' around 'social media'.

I've often heard that it's all about people taking photographs of their lunch, their dog, getting into rants online etc – and yes, that does happen. But move beyond the words 'social media', and instead consider just a few of the aspects it facilitates such as:

- customer engagement;
- customer communications;
- customer outreach and feedback;
- brand expression;
- thought leadership.

It is highly likely that the above concepts feel more grounded and worthwhile than perhaps 'social media'.

As we will explore in later chapters, it is important that we plan our social media activity effectively. For you as a leader, busy, time-strapped and with a focus on driving the business and prioritizing areas of commercial importance, then absolute clarity on why your organization is participating in social media, or indeed, why you are, is an important starting point. Doing social just because everyone else is – is not a robust strategy or reason to participate.

For CEOs or leaders who consider 'social media' as nothing more than a time-wasting, non-direct-revenue-generating distraction – whether that is your thinking or you are hoping to change someone else's thinking – opening your or their eyes to a wider focus and talking to yourself or to others of client and customer engagement, communication strategies, outreach and feedback strategies, can really help to bridge the gap between 'getting social' and the 'impact on the business'.

Social media channels are enablers – enablers to assist you to achieve necessary client, customer and new business engagement. Used as part of an integrated campaign or channel plan, they can steer or enhance activity. From an organizational or brand perspective, you may lead some activities via social channels, or you may plug in social media to support other channel activities.

As outlined in Chapter 2, there are more than 1 billion 'people' logging in to Facebook daily – and that's just Facebook: remember there are many other channels where people spend serious amounts of time. Some of them will be your customers or your potential customers. If social media is where your customers are, then shouldn't you be building these very channels into your communication and engagement plans? This includes your voice as thought leader or chief storyteller too.

As Brian J Dunn, former CEO of Best Buy told me: 'Social media is part of my life, not doing it is like saying communication doesn't fit into my schedule.'

If you have got stuck in your thinking of what social media is and why you don't do social media, I again ask you to consider some questions from a strategic perspective in order to assess any potential gaps where your social media activity could lead, steer or be integrated within:

- What is your customer engagement plan and programme?
- How do you actively listen to what customers are saying about you or your business?
- Where do you source ideas for relevant and engaging content?
- How do you engage those customers or prospective customers who are active on social channels?
- Is there a multi-channel integrated communications strategy in place?

To those who still think of 'social media' as activities that are not business critical, then simply stop calling it social media. Don't let the words blur the possibilities that these communication channels facilitate. There is always scope to reframe and rename if necessary.

Remember these three things

1   You don't have to do everything all at once. Start with one platform, find your rhythm and do it well. Then, if relevant – expand your activity.

2   As CEO or senior leader, you have the opportunity to be the chief storyteller.

3   Research findings state that over 80 per cent of people believe that leaders who are active on social media are better equipped to run a company.

Take action

As part of your 90-day plan in Chapter 7, we will focus on the 'how to' of each of these key Chapter 3 aspects:

- Consider your digital footprint. Assess where you are right now with your digital footprint, what it looks like, how you currently 'show up' and then take action to influence it so that what is out there is current and positions you as chief storyteller or key thought leader.

- Familiarize yourself with the tools available to you. Do some research into which channels and platforms are relevant for you. Review the useful apps on the GetSocial site.

- Sense check with others. If relevant, speak to your communications, social media team or agency to understand the organizational social media objectives and how your personal activity could align. Research and gain insights into what other leaders/CEOs are doing.

References

Blankfein, Lloyd (2011) [accessed 29 November 2017] CEO @GoldmanSachs, *Twitter* [Online] Twitter.com

Carvill, Michelle (2009) [accessed 29 November 2017] Founder @CarvillCreative | Digital Marketing & Social Media Pro | Author #GetSocial #BusinessofBeingSocial #socialCEO #yogakeepsmesane, *Twitter* [Online] Twitter.com

Carvill, M and Taylor, D (2015) *The Business of Being Social: A practical guide to harnessing the power of Facebook, Twitter, LinkedIn and YouTube for all businesses*, Crimson, London

Holmes, Ryan (2007) [accessed 29 November 2017] Entrepreneur, Investor, Future Enthusiast, Inventor, Hacker. Lover of Dogs, Owls and Outdoor Pursuits. Founder and CEO of Hootsuite. Support? @hootsuite_help, *Twitter* [Online] Twitter.com

Marques, Felipe (2017) [accessed 29 November 2017] How Blankfein Inspired BTG's CEO to Try Out Social Media, *Bloomberg Technology*, 10 November [Online] https://www.bloomberg.com/news/articles/2017-11-10/how-blankfein-inspired-btg-ceo-sallouti-to-try-out-social-media

04
Content

In Chapter 3 we looked at some of the most popular social media channels and tools to assist with optimizing communications, aligned with your digital brand and mindset.

Whilst understanding the channels and how they work and what you can get out of them is fundamental, a critical piece of getting social is the 'what' you are going to say and share.

I could write a whole book on content (and many have), and for good reason, as it is content that fuels your social media presence. As we will explore in this chapter, content takes many forms. Whether it's you sharing content that you or your organization have created from a thought leadership perspective, or content you have curated, either through listening in to your communities, influencers and audiences or perhaps just general conversation or a spontaneous moment – it's all content.

In keeping with the spirit of this book, my focus is on providing you with clarity of the where, what, when and how of content, together with a clear steer for practical implementation.

My content mantra is 'You are what you share'. Five simple words. But actually, when you give that sentence some thought, the implications are significant.

Without exception, in every workshop, every training course and every one-to-one I have ever engaged in, 'content' – and putting content out there – is where the majority of people feel most challenged.

Objections or concerns tend to look like this:

- 'I'm not naturally social.'
- 'What have I got to say?'
- 'No one wants to hear what I've got to say.'

- 'Our customers are too busy, they don't have time to engage.'
- 'There's so much out there, why would they want to listen to me?'
- 'What I do is private – I can't share what I'm doing.'
- 'I'm too busy to spend my time creating content.'
- 'I'm not a natural on camera.'
- 'I'm not a natural writer.'
- 'I leave communication to the experts.'
- 'I leave communication to the extraverts.'
- 'What if I say the wrong thing.'
- 'What if people don't like what I'm saying?'
- 'What if no one engages?'

I could go on…

Whether you relate to any of the above or not, I want to start by reassuring you that, when it comes to content, you are totally in control. During this chapter, my objective is to address some of those key objections – most of which, by the way, route back to 'fear'.

The thing to keep in mind is that, yes, consistency is important to keep your audiences tuned in, but authenticity and being useful totally trump consistency.

Content is a meaty topic so before we move on to strategy and pulling your plan together, I want us to look at the many aspects of content. We will also bring in to the chapter examples of what others are doing, so that you are equipped at the end of this chapter with enough insight, confidence and clarity to build your own practical content plan.

What you will learn from this chapter

- The role content plays for you as a 'social' leader.
- How to create content that creates connection.
- Useful content tips to optimize your social media activity.
- Creating a compelling and balanced content plan.

Let's also be clear when we set out into this chapter that whilst social media and content marketing strategies at an organizational level will no doubt include an aspect of assisting with search engine optimization (SEO), as a leader that is not what your content or social strategy is predominantly about. If your content happens to create any organic SEO benefits, then great, but your focus is not about keywords and content marketing, instead it is about sharing your voice, being transparent and authentic, humanizing the brand or business, and engaging and conversing with your audiences to build trust.

Everything is content

Content creation can at first seem like a huge task but, from a personal leadership perspective, where the greatest and most authentic content comes from is right from your day-to-day, real world.

As a leader, you steer, direct and make decisions daily. You are highly experienced and highly likely to be seen as a mentor or expert in your field. You understand strategy, business development and how to galvanize people to adapt and achieve. You have learnt from others and from first-hand experience.

From a micro perspective, in your working life you are creating content every day. In fact, we all are. Every conversation, every piece of advice you share, every decision you deliberate about and then make, every change you orchestrate or engineer, every policy, partnership or campaign you sign off, every opportunity for praise or reflection and every question you answer.

These day-to-day activities alone give you great opportunities to seed and develop content. Then, of course, there is the macro stuff going on around you.

World news, local news, sector news, organizational news and the impact it is having on your business or generally. Your opinion on anything topical. These areas, again, present an opportunity to develop engaging and purposeful content.

Quick exercise

Before we move on, reflect on the past 72 hours:

- What viewpoints have you shared?
- Which questions have you answered, either to your peers, team or customers?
- Which news items, articles or pages in books have you read with interest and perhaps scribbled notes in margins or on Post-it notes that could be used to inspire, educate or inform others?
- What conversations or debates have you had about something that chimes with your interests or values, either as a leader of or within your organization or, indeed, personally?
- What content have you shared internally with your team members that could be reframed and deemed useful by other audiences?
- Who have you met and where have you visited that could inspire an interesting or relevant topic to talk about?

That quick exercise is really just to get you thinking differently about the possibilities of content creation. Such real, slice-of-life insights brilliantly translate as authentic and engaging content, particularly when focused on either solving problems, sharing advice and insights or other aspects that matter to your audience. You are already in the perfect position to enable social media channels to become a natural extension of how you communicate.

Beware the curse of knowledge

You have to be mindful of the voice that jumps in saying… 'but everyone already knows about this. This isn't new, this isn't interesting or useful.' Beware of the 'curse of knowledge', which is assuming that others know what you know. We all do it. But in reality, they don't know what we know. Don't underestimate the value that your advice and viewpoint provides.

What that short exercise also illustrates is the fact that just by living day to day, that in itself presents opportunity for creating fresh, new content. There is also always opportunity to extend the life of a piece of content by repurposing it. Content that started out as a keynote, article or conversation can be broken down into personal quotes or memes, or even turned into a live-stream video.

It is about rethinking the possibilities of content generally, not only in the context of what seeds your content, but also how reusable a piece of content can be.

Know you, like you, trust you

When it comes to content creation, what matters to your audience(s) should always be a key consideration for the content you create.

If you are looking to create a connection that compels others to share your content, then formulaic content that reads like a scripted press release is not going to cut it.

Don't get me wrong, there is a place for promotional and PR-style content, but if you follow a simple 80/20 rule, then 80 per cent of your content should strive to be authentic, engaging, informative, useful, relevant and purposeful. Only 20 per cent (this is an absolute maximum) should be promotional. In fact, that is perhaps an acceptable baseline from an organizational level, but personally, from a leadership perspective, my preference would be to split that 95/5. After all, your focus is on amplifying brand values and building trusted relationships.

The best way to gain trust is to be open, authentic and honest. The more authentic your content is, the more people will trust it and engage with it and therefore, in turn, build trust and engage with you. Social programmes that are over-orchestrated, too polished and too programmatic, do not come across to readers as authentic. Content that does nothing but push promotional features and benefits of products or services, without adding in the conversational, human aspect, are totally missing the point and provide all who come across the content with clear evidence that such organizations clearly don't 'get' social.

The beauty of social media is that the channels are far freer than traditional communication channels. They invite real-time, one-to-one and one-to-many, two-way conversations. They therefore provide the opportunity to be creative and generous from a quality perspective with the content you create, using a range of media; whether text, video, live streaming or images. Importantly, they provide an opportunity for people to get to know you, like you and trust you.

Focusing a moment on trust. You will recall from the BrandFog 2016 research findings cited in Chapter 1, '82 per cent were more likely to trust a company whose leadership team engages with social media' (BrandFog, 2016). If we were to dig a little deeper into that research, my prediction is that from a content perspective, the trust is generated due to the human, personable real-world conversation and relationship development that social enables.

As John Legere, CEO, T-Mobile, advised when we spoke:

> What's the point of being on social if you are not going to be yourself? I'm the same person on social that I am running through Central Park. Just watch some of my live Periscope videos on Twitter! Part of what I love about social is that it's a conversation. It's not just about broadcasting stuff at people. It has to be a real two-way discussion. So, when people give you feedback, you show them you've heard them by doing something about it.
>
> I'm also a big believer in changing it up to keep things fresh. When I started Slow Cooker Sunday on Facebook Live, I knew it was a crazy thing for a CEO to do. But I like to put myself out there and share my passions – and you'll notice I even get some T-Mobile news in there. Over 1 million people now watch it each week. I had zero clue that so many people would tune in. I've had a blast doing it. But, more importantly, it gives me a whole new way to connect with people AND share the T-Mobile story.

Be brave, be bold, be true

When it comes to 'changing it up and keeping things fresh', in some respects I couldn't agree more with the point made by John (and indeed other leaders I interviewed), the point being that it's important to be brave, bold and true to yourself.

Through creative content, open and authentic conversation and emotional connection, John has created millions of social media followers who, as he explains in his interview, in a number of ways are having a positive impact on his business.

Social media has become ubiquitous with his role. Take a few minutes scanning his Twitter profile and you will see that from a 'personal brand' position he is very clear about the message he is sharing. He is the chief storyteller for the organization he leads, its brand champion, and his personality and personal brand are very apparent.

He makes it very clear what he stands for. His stance is consistent and one of being highly transparent both with team members and to the rest of the world. He is bold about sharing his values and when liaising directly with customers, and even calls out competitor performance.

But he also shares content around topical aspects and he's actually quite a useful person to follow for spotting new technological developments – so his curation is pretty interesting too. There is a blend of content:

- brand;
- entertainment;
- education;
- inspiration.

With his personal viewpoint, wrapped around each aspect.

From the perspective of humanizing the brand, through his online interactions John Legere offers a very personable and authentic experience. Whilst I've never worked with John and, actually, have never physically spoken to him (we did our interview digitally and communicated via direct messages over Twitter), I do actually feel that if I did personally meet him, I would pretty much know what to expect.

Such connectivity via social media is one of the key reasons social media works so well with managing customers and, at an organizational level, facilitates team collaboration. Even when distance divides people and it's not simple to centralize teams in one place, or service people face to face, social media connectivity assists with building relationships.

Another simple example of social media-building relationships I can personally recount to you is via Great Western Railways, the train service provider I use regularly. They, like most transport providers nowadays, have a Twitter account that I tune in to to keep up to date with what's happening with the train journey element of my commute. 'Ollie', who has been manning their social media customer service outpost for a few years now, is someone I myself, and indeed others on the commute, have never met. Yet the regular conversation we have with him has built a 'social' connection – to the end that myself and my fellow commuters regularly refer to and talk about 'what Ollie said' as if he is someone we know. He may even be a clever chat bot for all we know!

Content tells stories, content connects, but just as with any of the traditional channels, such as TV, billboard or radio, the social media channels are simply the enablers of your content.

The power that social media channels have, over and above traditional channels, is that they provide opportunity for people to instantaneously respond and react directly, and to share and amplify your content by simply hitting a button on a device that they pretty much carry around with them 24/7. Importantly, they provide a two-way conversation. It is not about simply broadcasting your message, but rather opening up the channel for conversation.

As mentioned previously, fear is a powerful emotion and a very real 'blocker'. Overcoming the fear of not being seen to have all the answers is a very real challenge, particularly for those in leadership positions. However, it is okay to have a conversation with someone and say: 'I'm not sure how to answer that', or 'I've never been asked about that before', or 'I'll have to have a think about that and come back to you.' After all, that's a totally natural and transparent response – and one you would give in a press conference or interview scenario. What you are showing with that type of response is that you don't have all the answers, and that you're real, human and honest, which in turn builds trust.

You are what you share

Therefore, what really matters to build relationships is not about how many channels you're 'on' but rather the 'what' that you pour into those channels.

It's the content you share that is the catalyst for starting relationships through which you can then continue to build trust and share of mind. Content serves you best when it is useful to those you are sharing it with and it forms part of a conversation.

The title of a blog post by the author Jay Baer, 'Why Content is Fire and Social Media is Gasoline', offers a simple, yet highly visual explanation of the relationship (Baer, 2014).

As you will witness from the experiences of CEOs and leaders in Chapter 8 and the Appendix, there are varying levels of participation when it comes to content creation. I urge you to look at one of the number of articles around the topic 'Top 100 CEOs on Social', and explore what others are doing. Simply google that term. A good reference is Conversocial's blog, 'The 10 Most Social Media-Minded CEOs' (Frumkin, 2017). In the article, you will find T-Mobile CEO, John Legere – in fact, you will find that John Legere is cited usually towards the top of most of such lists. For frequency and diversity of content, his activity is at the high end of the social spectrum.

Others cited in that top 10 article include Jack Salzwedel, CEO of American Family Insurance. Like John Legere, Jack uses social to have direct conversations with customers. Richard Branson, CEO of Virgin Group, is on the list too. He uses social to generate awareness around what's happening within the Virgin Group, and again, talks directly with customers. Much of his content is inspirational and motivational, in line with the spirit of the Virgin brand.

Bill Gates, co-founder of the Bill and Melinda Gates Foundation, uses social to champion social causes, using Twitter and other channels to educate and build awareness around areas such as disease and poverty. He also uses social to recognize and praise employees.

Sallie Krawcheck, CEO of Ellevest, uses social to advocate women in the workplace, as does Mary Barra, CEO of General Motors, discussing and empowering female leaders, and sharing news and spreading awareness of relevant initiatives such as 'Girls who Code', plus matters that are more indirectly related to the output of their businesses, and clearly close to their hearts, purpose and beliefs.

Tim Cook, CEO of Apple, uses social media extensively and posts in multiple languages, making a stance around communicating with global markets. He is also cited as the first Fortune 500 CEO to create a verified Weibo (Chinese equivalent of Twitter) account.

There are more examples cited in the article too: Elon Musk, CEO Tesla; Mark Bertolini, CEO Aetna; Gary Vaynerchuk, CEO Vaynerchuk Media. These are CEOs using social media each with their own purpose, be it brand building, building awareness around causes that matter to them, customer service or employee engagement, or a mix of all of these aspects. Each clearly sees the value in investing time being social.

Kevin Burrowes from PwC, one of the leaders I interviewed, is also active, tuning in daily to catch up with relevant activity on Twitter. By his own admission, he is aware that on the content front there is more he could be doing. But even though he may not be right up there on the top of 'most active' users and hitting the 'lists', he is currently doing what works for him. That is still more than many of his peers, and far more active than many of those 60 per cent of 'CEOs' cited in the findings by Weber Shandwick in Chapter 1, who, whilst having created a presence on social media, are doing absolutely nothing with it.

Quality over quantity

This brings up the frequency question. In short, the quality of your content and the opportunity it has for being purposeful and useful for others trumps the volume of content you put out.

Once upon a time, it was all about volume, consistently feeding the social media network algorithms with keyword-enabled content on a daily basis. Such demand was met with a total saturation of highly keyword-enabled, yet mediocre or poor-quality content.

Fortunately, those algorithms have significantly changed. In short, it is wiser to take the time to deliver less yet more engaging, stickier content than churning out content for the sake of it.

Content rhythms that work for you

The key to remember is that you are not a robot, you are a busy human being. Finding your content rhythm is all about what works for you. There will be times when it is important to focus on creating fireworks (let's call that the wow content) and sparklers (still as satisfying but not as big a production), but then the majority of time you will be fine with simply keeping throwing the logs on the fire. I love this analogy of fireworks, sparklers and logs, from John Willshire, founder of strategic design agency Smithery. We'll use this further in a moment.

For example, I target myself to share thought leadership pieces at least once a month, sometimes more often, depending on what I'm working on and whether it naturally lends itself to sharing. However, in our time-strapped worlds, when committing time to write a book, I tend to focus attention on the content for the book over finding the time to generate thought leadership pieces. This doesn't mean I don't continue with social activity, it just means I pull back from my thought leadership 'firework, sparkler' style content and instead spend most of my time focused on throwing logs on the fire, interacting, engaging, sharing viewpoints, images, a few live videos etc. Does it mean I'm not as useful? Possibly, but even if it's not directly my content that is providing advice, I still endeavour to share posts with useful links or answer questions and direct people to someone or something I'm aware of that may assist. I am still part of the community and I am still engaging and participating.

Overall, your content creation will go through peaks and troughs. However, the freer and more organic you are, making content work for you, rather than you working for it, the better all round.

This may be very different from a corporate brand perspective, where there is a very fixed content plan, but for your own personal perspective people are more interested in what you are up to and what you have got to say on matters, than necessarily expecting you to be an expert content creator.

Putting your viewpoint at the heart of content offers the opportunity to share your industry expertise and positions you as a thought leader. Sharing that content on social media offers the opportunity to extend the reach of that content, opening up channels to facilitate conversation and engagement.

Determine your message

A common theme cited by the leaders and CEOs I interviewed is the importance of being yourself and authentic activity. However, aligned with being authentic, there is the key aspect of having clarity on why you are participating on social media in the first place.

Answering the question 'What's your purpose for being on social media?' will assist you with gaining clarity on the type of content you create. However, your purpose may vary. For example:

- Is your main aim to tune in and be there to speak directly with customers?
- Are you there to showcase changes you are making within the organization?
- Perhaps as an organization you are passionate about making a difference in a particular area and is it that difference that you are going to champion?
- Is it perhaps to set the record straight and to ensure that your organization's voice is heard from an authoritative source on a particular aspect?
- Is your focus on supporting and aligning with organizational campaigns?
- Is it about rebuilding reputation and gaining trust?

Understanding the purpose is important as it helps to drive the type and style of content you will be sharing, particularly in the early days.

We will look at content planning in a while but, for now, keeping your audience front and centre, consider the following questions:

- What is my message?
- What is my authentic voice?
- What am I looking to achieve?
- What content is going to fit with my purpose?
- What content is going to be useful to my audience?
- What questions have they raised?
- What do they want to know about?
- What do I want them to know about?
- What do we get asked all the time?
- What is important to them?

Understanding your 'why' assists with steering your 'what'

There may be a very clear linear focus for your social media presence, or indeed it may include many different interrelated aspects. Regardless, it is clear that understanding your 'why' assists with steering your 'what'.

To showcase this away from some of the CEOs and leaders highlighted in Chapter 8, I have been following a millennial CEO, Jack Parsons, CEO of Big Youth Group. The business, and therefore Jack, is 'on a mission to improve the odds for young people'. The purpose is very clear, and you will find relevant messages on Jack's personal social media outposts and the social media outposts for the Big Youth Group.

The focus of the content is all around delivering on their purpose. On Twitter there are videos, interviews, images and interactions. Just as in real-world conversations, his interactions are varied, from responding to people who are tweeting him to thank him for being so inspirational, with a simple thank you, to liaising with other influencers or CEOs who have shared a relevant post, which Jack has commented on. Or providing inspiration and answering questions to his direct audience, the teens and young entrepreneurs, around the skills needed to survive the changing world of work; retweeting photos of him meeting others or sharing PR pieces; video interviews from Grant Thornton or podcasts via City AM. It's a stream of what is happening with Jack's mission.

On LinkedIn, his articles all focus on the same mission and provide 'thought leadership' advice and content around the topic. Of course, he is on Snapchat and Instagram too, sharing live stories of what's happening during his day, and the progress he is making.

Striking a balance

Getting clarity on your purpose, your mission and your message is a worthy exercise, and it is likely that it will align with the same core values of your organization, or it may take a slightly different slant or focus. In the case of Mary Barra, CEO of General Motors, her content focuses not solely on what GM is up to but, as the first female CEO of an automobile company, on championing women in the workplace and empowering female leaders.

Once you have figured out what you are aiming to achieve out on the channels, it is important to keep in mind that the purpose of your content is to engage people so that they feel inspired to comment, follow your channels, like or share your content, advocating and amplifying the reach of your message into their audiences.

We will look at metrics in Chapter 5 in more detail, but such actions as sharing and commenting give you an indication that your content is meaningful and useful to the communities you're building.

As you will witness from the experiences of CEOs and leaders in Chapter 8, there are varying levels of participation. John Legere is at the extreme end of the spectrum, highly active on a number of channels with a variety of mixed media content.

The number of channels you choose to participate on, and the level of activity, will determine your content requirements. As to the type of content you share, when working with clients, I refer to a simple framework to assist with balance:

40% Curated	30% Repurposed	20% Created	10% Spontaneous
Curating and sharing others' content that you find interesting or relevant. (Of course, you can always add your own personal twist to this – for example, by adding a comment when retweeting something.)	Repurposing and recycling content you already have. • Blog posts – turning written posts into live streams or vice versa • Keynotes • Articles • Interviews	Your unique content. Thought leadership pieces. • New blog posts • New articles • Live streams • Video • Interviews • Product launches • Campaigns • Keynotes	Leaving space in your content pipeline for spontaneous slice-of-life content. Sharing real-world relevant stuff as it happens.

As you can see from the framework, it simply breaks down content into either repurposing content that you already have, developing fresh content or curating content from others, keeping some space free for spontaneous messaging.

Whilst I have broken it down into these segments, the percentages are not prescriptive and are likely to change. It is really to provide you with a steer on how you can map out different types of content.

As mentioned earlier, I personally like the concept reference of 'fireworks, sparklers and logs on the campfire', which I heard from John Willshire, founder of strategic design agency Smithery. This simple model provides a way to segment content in line with a highly visual analogy. However, the take on the type of content in each category is my own – John's view on what that content is may differ.

Fireworks, sparklers and logs on the campfire

Fireworks 'Firework' content refers to content that makes a lot of noise and attracts significant attention.

It is likely to be more in-depth in the planning and potentially more expensive to produce, encompassing for example more highly produced video, or longer-form thought leadership papers and guides, resources or research findings reports. If all content was a constant stream of fireworks, it would most definitely become overwhelming to produce. Plus, another consideration is that the objective of your 'firework' content is to create a bit of 'wow' factor, whereas too much would, over time, create an expectation that would dilute the impact.

Sparklers 'Sparkler' content refers to content that is central to what your organization or you do, and that you can keep using. It is still engaging but is also simpler to put together. I refer to this as 'evergreen' content. It is content that does not really change. It isn't necessarily about being topical or creating wow, but rather is at the heart of what your organization is about. This may include brand value pieces, 'how to' stories, FAQs, about us stories, or content about how and where it all started. It is unlikely that this will form the bulk of your content sharing. But it's there for you to draw upon periodically, when you need it.

Logs on the campfire 'Logs on the campfire' content refers to day-to-day content. This may include thought leadership articles, blog posts (or indeed these may be pushed into your Sparklers category). It could also encompass curated content, sharing what others have said, perhaps with your viewpoint attached. This is natural slice-of-life content that keeps your personal brand glowing. It is usually the bulk of the content you will be sharing.

Again, as with the 40/30/20/10 mapping, there is no specific prescription as to how you 'blend' your types of content. You have to find and then do what works for you, but generally, the ratio will look something like: 1 firework to 5 sparklers to 20 logs on the fire.

Fear of saying the wrong thing

As we have explored so far in this chapter, you have the opportunity to become chief storyteller both internally and externally in your leadership role. Along with reframing how you think of content creation, you also need to reframe your thinking about what you share.

In the previous chapter, we talked about you stepping out of your metaphorical comfort zone and getting out into the garden to join the conversations. The content you share may indeed become part of those conversations, but in certain scenarios it is going to be the catalyst for conversation.

Saying the wrong thing happens. But when you say the wrong thing on potentially far-reaching social media channels there is not only the possibility of significant amplification, but also the opportunity for people to reply and share their view directly. Here lies the dilemma of being 'authentically' you on social.

I'm afraid there is no magic formula or tried-and-tested model to advise you which way to manage this. It is about sharing and behaving in a way that works for you, your personal brand and your organization's brand.

There is always opportunity to hold your hands up and act in a transparent and open way. In fact, when crisis hits, all anyone really wants is clear leadership and open communication. For leaders who have taken that stance in the past, it has worked in their favour. Joel Gascoigne, CEO of Buffer, is an example of this. When Buffer was hacked, rather than keeping quiet he came out and tackled the crisis head on, giving customers actionable advice and using his and Buffer's social media presence to keep people informed and have direct conversations. Honest, open and transparent.

Kevin Burrowes, Head of Clients and Markets at PwC, in his interview told me that the most challenging aspect of being engaged with social media is:

> Getting the balance right between being personal and corporate can sometimes be a challenge. I often see people on Twitter having a rant about something frustrating that has happened, but it wouldn't be professional for me to do that in my role and could have some serious implications.
>
> You've always got to think about what you're saying and what the impact of that could be. Remember too that old posts are stored and available for anyone to see if your profiles are open; there have been several examples in the news recently where people have been caught out with inappropriate or unprofessional Twitter posts from several years ago. My rule is: if you have even the slightest doubt about what you want to say, don't post it.

Regardless of whether, like Kevin, you are in the world of professional services or not, finding the balance can be a very real challenge. It is about knowing the boundaries that you feel comfortable with and making a call.

Respect and common sense go a long way in business, whether online or offline. The simple rule of 'if you don't want to see it published, don't say it', is a good one.

Caron Bradshaw, CEO, Charity Finance Group (CFG), told me:

> A lot of people I've spoken to (particularly those who are not big social media users) are scared about the risks associated with putting out content that hasn't gone through a rigorous process and scrutiny. I see it more as an extension to less formal communications that you might have, say, at a networking event. You use judgement on what to share and what not to say, you engage in positive conversations and walk away from those that are going nowhere and you definitely don't hit the wine!

Be yourself

Whilst some leaders and CEOs work with either their PA or social media or communication teams to assist them with content creation and planning out their social media activity, there is a clear message that comes through in all the interviews I've conducted to date – and that is to be sure you are doing the bulk of the messaging and engagement yourself. It has to be your voice.

The more authentic and less 'managed' your activity is and the less jargon and the more real-world conversation, the more relatable. That said, when it comes to the planning and management of your content, you can and most definitely should involve others.

Content planning

The 40/30/20/10 balance and the fireworks, sparklers, logs on the campfire concepts help you with some ideas relating to the amount and type of content you share.

Of course, it is also useful to consider the purpose of those content pieces too. For example, if developing a new video, is the purpose to educate, entertain, inspire or promote? Are you looking for emotional connection or to build awareness?

If we break down content into these areas again, it provides you with some ideas relating to the purpose of your content:

Entertain	Educate	Inspire	Promote
• Competitions	• Guides	• Interviews with influencers	• Case studies
• Games	• E-books	• Reviews	• Product features and benefits
• Fun viral videos	• Thought leadership articles	• Testimonials	
• Quizzes	• Reports	• Keynote video/slides	• Promotional offers
• Keynote video/slides	• Press releases	• Content that inspires you that you feel compelled to share	
	• How to/demos		
	• Keynote video/slides		

For example, going back to Jack Parsons and the content he is sharing, from the 'Inspire' column: he is sharing content from interviews with Grant Thornton around being chosen as one of their 'Faces of a Vibrant Community' campaign. There are inspirational tweets daily, encouraging and motivating those he is targeting; curation of relevant articles that others have shared that he is resharing, and adding his own comments to; interviews with CEOs and HR leads within organizations about what they are looking for from their employees – educating his audience as to the skills required.

From a 'Promote' perspective, he shares his cause 'to improve the odds for young people'. He encourages both organizations and youths to join the cause, promoting links to sign up to the website, sharing features and benefits of his campaign, the task in hand and his purpose.

In some cases, the purpose of a piece of content may be absolutely crystal clear to determine, but it is not always the case. For example, the keynote could be entertaining, educational and inspirational. A competition may focus on entertainment value, but also be hugely educational around teaching someone how to use a product, which in turn is promotional.

The key is not to create rigid silos from which to select, but rather to illustrate that there is plenty of opportunity to mix up the content you share.

Food for thought on thought leadership

Going back to Chapter 1 and Edelman's 2017 Trust Barometer, if you read the full report, it talks of the declining trust, not only of CEOs but across the political landscape, news and overall reporting of facts.

In line with exploring the impact of thought leadership and trust, Edelman ran another study relating to the impact of thought leadership in the B2B arena. Edelman and LinkedIn surveyed 1,300 business decision makers and C-suite executives on how thought leadership influences their own purchase behaviour. The article, 'Is Thought Leadership Earning or Losing Business Decision Makers' Trust?' shares the findings (Day, 2017):

- 82 per cent said that thought leadership increased their trust in an organization.

- 84 per cent said they valued thought leadership that was forwarded by someone they know and respect.

- 68 per cent said they valued thought leadership that was forwarded by their bosses.

When those surveyed were asked what they wanted from thought leadership:

- 79 per cent said they wanted thought leadership to identify new trends or issues they should know about.

- 66 per cent said they wanted more data, charts, infographics, key facts and figures.

- The overall desire was for the content to be short. The preferred method is short-form three- to four-page documents, snackable media that can be digested in one or two minutes, and short-form videos.

The other key finding from the study, which is not to be ignored, is that building trust and credibility through content is not to be underestimated from a commercial perspective. Thought leadership was twice as effective at winning business than the creators thought.

With those content aspects in mind, let's look at a simple way of breaking down those ideas and concepts into a practical content plan.

Developing your content plan

Step 1: what's happening in your world?

A good place to start is by mapping out what happens in your world as a leader, such as the activities, launches, promotions, events, trade shows, speaking engagements, analysis and reports. There will be activities that you are well aware of in advance. These activities give you an opportunity to consider what content is going to be relevant for you to prepare or engage with:

Month	Your Activity	Organization Activity	General/ Seasonal
January	Speaking engagement – Japan		
February	Radio interview	New product launch	Valentine's Day
March	Budget review		International Women's Day
April	Quarterly analysis review/report		
May		Big promotional campaign begins	
June	ABC Expo Madrid – keynote		
July	Quarterly analysis review/report		
August	Judging ABC awards selecting shortlist		
September	Suppliers forum	Big promotional campaign ends	
October	ABC Awards Event – sponsoring	New office opening in Spain	
November	Internal forecast report	Recruitment drive	
December			Holiday season

Whilst such long-form planning is by no means the sum total of everything that is likely to happen throughout the year, what it illustrates is that there are aspects that you may do regularly for you to consider as part of your content planning.

For example: to illustrate the point, let's look at the scenario of planning on delivering a keynote in Madrid in June. It is likely the Expo would have its own social activity going on around the event, and most likely a dedicated #hashtag has been created to collate all the relevant conversations:

- Tune in and follow the Expo hashtag to see who is talking about attending and what people are saying.

- Where relevant, reply to any that mention that they are looking forward to hearing you speak.

- Share tweets saying that you are looking forward to talking all things 'ABC' at the Expo – who is coming along? Use the event #hashtag in your tweets to connect to the wider conversation.

- Create a short talking-head video or Instagram Live or Facebook Live – a teaser introducing what you will be talking about and what you are looking forward to seeing.

- Connect with other keynote speakers or relevant businesses that will be attending. Say hello – looking forward to the opportunity to meet.

- Share real-world images: 'Working on my presentation for the ABC Expo in June. 10 more days to go! #ABCexpo'.

- On the day(s) of the Expo, stream live video via Twitter, Facebook, LinkedIn or Instagram (any channels that are relevant to you).

- Add images or video to your 'Story' if using relevant channels (Instagram, Snapchat, Facebook).

- Follow the #hashtag and respond to any relevant tweets, or just generally keep an eye on what is developing.

- When people mention you or your talk or your brand, respond. Join the conversation.

- Post event – create a longer-form thought leadership piece around what you got out of the Expo, who you met, some of your favourite moments, talks and key takeaways. Tag people you mention – so they will see the post and have a prompt to read and share it.

- Tweet that article, using the Expo #hashtag. Again, tag relevant people/brands in your tweets.

- If relevant, do a live talking head about the same topic, what happened at the event, key takeaways, favourite talks.

- Thank your team and the organizers for such a great event. Great to be part of it. Thanks for having me, etc.

- Share the presentation, if relevant, on slideshare, share it via your LinkedIn profile.

- Tweet the links.

- Throughout the event, take live pics: your team, the event, talks, slides.

As you can see from the above ideas, the opportunities to utilize content from just this one scenario are vast.

Step 2: what is happening in your organization's world?

Just as there will be activities fixed and planned in for your own personal activity, if your organization is already engaged with social, then there is likely to be a content strategy or content calendar in place, aligning with key launches or activities.

If there isn't, then you may want to raise the question as to how the content aspect of your organization's social activity is being managed. Reviewing what is going on at the organizational macro level from a communications, marketing and social media activity and campaign perspective, enables you to align your activity to support and amplify, where relevant.

In John Legere's interview, he told me that he plans some content with teams relating to the bigger campaigns (think fireworks), but then the bulk of it is down to talking to customers and team members (think logs on the campfire). In the case of Kevin Burrowes, he mentions that he sits down each month with his PA and they review his diary and discuss and decide what he plans to do that month via LinkedIn and Twitter (sparklers and logs on the campfire).

Dr Sam Collins will share content to complement and align with what is happening at Aspire, and Caron Bradshaw advises that whilst CFG's content is most definitely planned by the communications team, and she will of course tweet or share links to amplify that content, her own social activity is far less choreographed than CFG's, and whilst not chaotic or unstructured, she likens it to 'improv': freedom within structure.

Caron also told me that she gets support from her communications team in other ways too. For example, they help her create short-form versions of content for use in the online channels and they are there in an advisory capacity for Caron to liaise with when she is unsure whether difficult topics may be sensible for her to engage with.

Caron advises that she may have blog posts part drafted or structured for her for expedience. However, for the most part, she writes her own content. 'It is important that my words have my voice.'

Step 3: what is happening generally? What's topical, what's seasonal?

Other aspects for you to consider when thinking about your content plan are aspects such as national holidays, special days celebrated in your country, by your organization, and seasonality in general. Again, these provide you with topical and relevant talking points.

In fact, there is a 'special day' for everything now. Google 'Days of the Year Calendar' and you will find a selection of calendars that showcase an eclectic mix of global celebrations.

Strive to make content a habit

In Chapter 3 we looked at the social channels and the type of content best suited for each channel.

As well as building in the social channels, or the ones you choose to participate on, into your content calendar, don't forget to include your corporate channels too, such as your website, company blog and intranet as well as any other internal communication channels you may utilize.

On the www.getsocial.site, in the resources section, I have shared a spreadsheet that is set up for 60 days of activity, which includes tabs for your personal activity, your organizational activity, relevant topical/general activity, and also has a colourful key chart relating to the type of content and channel. It is there to assist you with mapping your content for your 90-day plan (which we'll get to in Chapter 7).

In the meantime, let's finish this chapter by looking at some practical content pointers.

Content tips

- When curating, always read an article before sharing it on your channels, and include a reason for sharing it. Sharing it is effectively advocating the content. Just because the headline looks topical or on point, doesn't mean that the body of the piece follows through. Plus, people will be looking to you to advise them as to why you think it is worthy of sharing. Remember, it is your reputation at stake, so do the groundwork, take a read and be confident in what it is you are sharing, and then help others to engage by telling them why. It may be as simple as including something along the lines of 'good read', 'agree with this', or 'excellent point' in the comments. This way, even though it is not your content, you are still being helpful by helping others to filter out the good stuff and cut through the noise.

- If you are curating and sharing someone else's content it is good practice to either tag them or cite them. In fact, tagging them on social media alerts them to the fact that you have shared it, which in some cases is used as a tactic for igniting a conversation or a connection.

- Sometimes it is easier to be interviewed and then repurpose that content into a number of outposts. That might include quotes, short video soundbites or tweets, even transcribed as a LinkedIn article.

- No man is an island, particularly when it comes to content creation. Get relevant team members involved, and not just your marketing and communications teams. You will be surprised where great ideas and creativity are sparked from. Those on the front line in your customer service team can have brilliant insights to share.

- If a content idea pops into your head, capture it. If you don't capture it when it's looming, it is almost guaranteed that it will disappear. I can't count the number of times I think, 'that would make a really useful blog topic', and then the day goes by and I've lost it. Capturing is the first step to creating. Notebook or notes app, either way, be sure to jot down those ideas.

- Commit to starting a blog or regularly contributing an article to your organization's website or to LinkedIn's Pulse publishing platform. Disciplining yourself to regularly writing thought leadership longer-form content creates a good basis to develop a content-creating habit to fuel your social media activity.

Remember these three things

1 Listen. Always be listening.

2 For content ideas, frequently asked questions or email themes you find yourself repeatedly sharing are good places to source your content ideas. Some of the best content that engages others is when it is solving a problem of theirs. Speak to your teams too and find out common issues that arise. If you have a front-line customer service team, engage them too; they are a goldmine of information.

3 The more authentic and less 'managed' your activity is, and the less jargon and more real-world conversation, the more relatable.

Take action

As part of your 90-day plan in Chapter 7, we will focus on the 'how to' of each of these key Chapter 4 aspects:

- Attack your content plan. Review content that you already have and determine how it can be updated or repurposed to extend or resurrect its life. Can a thought leadership long-form piece be turned into snackable two-minute videos? This is an iterative process. If the message is evergreen, then this provides you with opportunity to share the message in various formats over periods of time. Set up meetings with relevant teams – for example, your communications team, your customer service team and your leadership team. Find out what is going on in the business from a content/thought leadership perspective. Tune in. Review what's happening in your world and what's topical.

- Block out time in your diary for content creation or capture. Start with 15 minutes twice a week to capture ideas and an hour for creation. It won't just magically happen unless you set aside time to make it happen.

- Review the social media guidelines within your organization, then be sure to familiarize yourself with what is suggested regarding content, tone of voice and brand messaging. On reflection, you may find they need some editing. Either way, familiarize yourself and commit to leading by example as a key storyteller for the organization.

References

Baer, Jason (2014) [accessed 29 November 2017] Why Content is Fire and Social Media is Gasoline [Blog] *Convince & Convert with Jay Baer*, 7 May [Online] http://www.convinceandconvert.com content-marketing/why-content-is-fire-and-social-media-is-gasoline/

BrandFog (2016) [accessed 29 November 2017] CEO, Social Media, Brand Reputation and Brand Trust Survey [Online] http://brandfog.com/ BRANDfog2016CEOSocialMediaSurvey.pdf

Day, Stephen (2017) [accessed 29 November 2017] Is Thought Leadership Earning or Losing Business Decision Makers' Trust? [Blog] *LinkedIn Marketing Solutions Blog*, 1 June [Online] https://business.linkedin. com/marketing-solutions/blog/marketing-for-tech-companies/2017/ is-thought-leadership-earning-or-losing-business-decision-makers

Frumkin, Tamar (2017) [accessed 29 November 2017] The 10 Most Social Media Minded CEOs [Blog] *Conversocial*, 10 February [Online] http:// www.conversocial.com/blog/the-10-most-social-media-minded-ceos

05
Your personal social media strategy

Given that the intent of this book is to steer you, the leader, in developing your social media activity, in this chapter, from a strategy development perspective, I address your personal social media strategy.

In Chapter 6, we will then look at organizational social media strategy, which for you as a leader may be something you direct, steer, contribute towards, or perhaps are keen to develop. Given that organizational strategy and personal strategy are inextricably linked, then there may be a bit of crossover, but the key outcome is that you have clarity on what you are going to focus on, and how your activity aligns with overall business objectives.

Before we move further into the chapter, I want us to reflect a little about social media. Let's take a few moments to consider just why it has been embraced and adopted at such pace.

Social media, social networks, social communications, social technologies or social web, however you wish to label the channels and what they appropriate, 'social' has well and truly hit a tipping point where use for business (and indeed for many other aspects), is widely accepted. To understand why, let's start with the basic human aspect that we are simply social creatures who crave social interaction. After all, remember, solitary confinement is a punishment.

Thousands of years ago we gathered in groups around campfires to share stories and experiences. Whilst the world and technology has moved on and changed, our inherent design has not. Our desire for 'tribal' social interaction remains. Today, technology has enabled us to gather in tribes around social media networks whenever it suits us. Regardless of time or distance, the social media networks enable connectivity – within your organization, personally and beyond.

I myself am a member of a number of 'groups' where participants regularly speak and share experiences. In most cases I have never personally met the majority of the people in the group. However, as a member of the group (or community) I have committed time and energy not only to tune in and listen to the viewpoints of others but, where I feel I have something to contribute, to get engaged and develop relationships.

The connection is still real and the usefulness of many of these virtual relationships is just as significant as if they were colleagues or clients I collaborate with face to face. Importantly, provided there is an internet connection, I can choose to connect at any time I want and in the way I choose.

When you strip it back, social media is fairly straightforward. The channels and technologies allow one-to-one, one-to-many and many-to-many connection; they are effectively the platforms, the infrastructure, the enablers.

Content or 'media' is the 'what' or the message we share, and as we explored in the previous chapter, that content can take many forms and meet many purposes. It is effectively the 'interaction' taking place within the infrastructure.

For ease, let's liken it to another type of infrastructure, let's say plumbing. The pipes are all interlinked to enable the free flow of water to provide resource to relevant areas to serve a purpose. The infrastructure is the plumbing system, the enabler, and the water flowing through is the interaction.

Like all infrastructures, things tend to work better when all the cogs are moving in the right direction. This also applies to social media across the business. As we will touch on in this chapter and in more detail in the next chapter, 'social media is not an island'. When social media is streamlined across the business, with everyone clearly informed, pulling together and steering in the same direction to deliver on shared objectives, then that is when great returns are realized.

What you will learn from this chapter

- Why it makes sense to align your personal activity with business objectives.
- How to define your personal objectives and personal brand.
- Determining objectively driven ROI metrics.
- Simple tactics for practical execution, understanding and measuring progress.

Nothing has changed, yet everything has changed

As we have heard in previous chapters, being 'social' is fundamentally focused on building relationships and connecting. Social networking in the true sense of those words.

Social media aligns well with business, as whilst we may measure the success of the business by the bottom line, rather than how engaged it is with its people or customers, most certainly a key driver for the health of that bottom line relates to the strength of that connection and the efficiencies and complexities of connecting customers with the brand, the products, the service, as well as connecting employees with each other, the business, the brand and customers.

Connection and relationships have always mattered in business and so, from that perspective, nothing has changed. However, the dynamics of such connections have changed.

Social media technologies have enabled freedom from time and distance and the opportunity to remove often strangulating, fixed silos, enabling connection to flow more freely and more speedily across divisions.

The channels in and of themselves are really relatively simple. Once you have learnt about the technologies and the shortcuts, then like all technology, it is just a case of keeping on top of the innovation and iterations.

The real challenge with 'being social' relates not to technology, but rather, shifting peoples' mindsets, change management and creating new habits. It's doing things differently. Of course, scaling technologies throughout large corporations provides its own structural challenges, and we will look further into this in Chapter 6.

The truth is, like anything transformational, it takes effort, time, commitment, learning, optimization and iteration.

Changing habits, mindsets, belief systems and fears

Bringing the above back to you, the same applies. You will potentially be changing the way you do things. It will take some effort, some time, some learning and some commitment.

Being active on social media or getting social media, whilst at first may be something you intentionally 'do', fundamentally, you want it to become something you 'are' – an extension of you and your everyday role.

In fact, when you take a look through the full interviews in the Appendix, without exception, pretty much every leader mentions the point that social media has become intrinsically entwined with their 'business as usual'. Whilst that may not be where you are right now, that is where we are heading, and indeed customer and organizational demands are also part of the steering committee.

Be objectively driven

Effectively, your organization's business strategy is steered by objectives. For you by association, as a leader within that business, those same objectives drive your focus.

Whilst the first few chapters of this book have provided you with reasons as to why it is becoming increasingly important for leaders and CEOs to engage with and embrace social media and social technologies, it is still critical not to get caught up in the foray and simply dive in just because everyone else is doing so.

For just shy of a decade I have worked with organizations and people helping them to onboard, engage and optimize social media activity. In those early days, the people who saw potential and really 'got' social media were most certainly in the minority. There were many conversations with leaders where social media was considered the latest fad, all hype and no substance and part of a bubble that would burst.

Well, here we are, present day and, of course, social media is now a fundamental part of how people communicate – as individuals, within organizations and with customers, partners and suppliers.

However, scepticism still remains. Whenever I hold a talk or run a workshop with a group and I ask some general ice-breaker questions about who is on social media and who is still sceptical, to date there is still a show of hands by those bold sceptics. Considerably less, but nevertheless, there is still scepticism. The reality is that, with any change, we all adapt at different rates.

From a number of my experiences, I've gleaned that the reason for scepticism traces back not necessarily to different rates of adaption or adoption, but rather to people not understanding the value that social media brings to the business. This is largely down to a very basic planning flaw by people and organizations: not setting relevant and purposeful objectives at the outset.

Effectively, by not plugging social media into the business from an objectively driven perspective, it doesn't provide any opportunity for social media to prove its true value.

Social media is not an island

When social media strategy is executed in a silo, there tends to be an overfocus on what I shall refer to as 'vanity' outcomes. These are outcomes that focus on activities relating to growing the number of followers or gaining more engagement, likes or shares.

Don't get me wrong, growing your audience is an important part of generating more 'reach', and it is important to do that. However, such activities are not strategy, they are tactics used to serve a specific purpose. The purpose for growing followers or gaining more engagement should be clearly defined and tied into delivering on key business objectives.

Determining strategic objectives for the growth and development of the business is no easy task. There are overarching business objectives and those objectives then cascade to every relevant business unit, theoretically aligning organizational efforts. Each department is either tasked with or develops their own objectives, designed to support the overall business objectives.

When social media was initially adopted within organizations, it usually sat within the marketing division and largely focused on outbound, broadcast media. Social media channels were seen as just another way to push messages out to audiences, replicating the traditional broadcast methods (billboard, TV, press, direct mail, advertising), which was what all organizations had been doing for years and years.

However, over the years, the merits of social media – such as two-way, real-time conversations, one-to-one and one-to-many conversations, real-time tuning in and listening to audiences or building loyal, engaged communities – have been realized.

Such people-to-people, relationship-building elements have led to social media being leveraged as a resource beyond marketing, to support a range of business units to deliver their objectives. As illustrated in Figure 5.1, social media is being used across a number of business units strategically and tactically.

In my view, the question should not be 'How do we build a social media strategy?' but rather 'How can we use social media and social technologies to help us deliver our business objectives?'

Figure 5.1 Plugging in social media across the organization

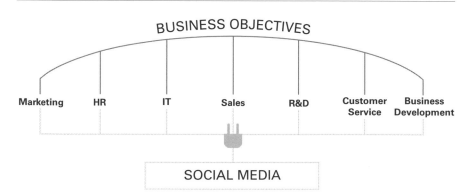

For your personal strategy, aligning your activity is also key. The question remains exactly the same: 'How do I use social media to deliver against our business objectives?'

I love the saying by Zig Ziglar: 'Those that aim for nothing, hit it with remarkable accuracy.' Nowhere truer does that chime than with social media.

If you make your social media activity objectively driven, then your why, your message, your content, the what you are tuning into and identifying what you need to measure, becomes far clearer. With this in mind, let's walk through each step of the Smart Social Focus Model, as illustrated in Figure 5.2.

Please note that the steps within the model are iterative and the order is not prescriptive. How you approach these can and will change as your activity evolves. That dot in the middle of the star is either you, or your organization, and you can pivot according to requirements.

Figure 5.2 Smart Social Focus Model

Plan

Passionate about making things happen and getting things done, I'm a big believer that there is no better way to get started than to get started. Sometimes, we can overthink things and become paralyzed by over analysis.

As discussed earlier in the chapter, embarking in social media activity simply because it is about time you did, or you feel you should, is not the smartest way to 'get social'.

In fact, it is often the lack of focused attention aligning social media to support organizational objectives that causes challenges and manifests scepticism, particularly when it comes to measuring ROI, which we will explore in greater detail later in the chapter.

To illustrate the point, let's consider a simple illustration. I like to keep things simple, so I'll refer to objectives as 'the what' and tactics as 'the how'.

Business objective – (the what):
Increase the number of new customers by 10 per cent by end of Q2.

With the objective clarified and target and time period applied, such an objective can be disseminated business-wide to sales, marketing, R&D, IT, customer service, business development etc. In their own way, or in some cases collaboratively, each division will develop strategies and tactics to impact the desired outcome.

Whilst, traditionally, social media may have once upon a time sat purely in marketing, and indeed may still sit in one division, or have its own division, the insights and merits expand beyond one division.

Each business unit cascades the overarching business objective, developing their own 'what' and 'how' and illustrating where social media 'plugs in' to objectives and impacts tactics:

Marketing

- Objectives:
  - brand awareness *(social media plugs in here)*;
  - building loyalty *(social media plugs in here)*;
  - expanding reach *(social media plugs in here)*.

- Tactics and activities impacted by social media:
  - promotional broadcast channel;
  - paid-for social media advertising campaigns to amplify reach;
  - targeting specific granular demographics;
  - real-time tracking resource;
  - competitor tracking;
  - sentiment tracking;
  - research;
  - business intelligence;
  - influencer outreach.

Sales

- Objectives:
  - expand customer base into new territories *(social media plugs in here)*;
  - expand demographic profiles *(social media plugs in here)*.

- Tactics and activities impacted by social media:
  - business intelligence;
  - research tool tracking real-time activity;
  - insights for a more informed consultative sales approach;
  - targeting demographics and behavioural patterns;
  - relationship development and nurture tool;
  - competitor tracking.

Customer service

- Objectives:
  - brand awareness *(social media plugs in here)*;
  - brand reputation management *(social media plugs in here)*;
  - building customer loyalty *(social media plugs in here)*;
  - increase customer satisfaction and happiness *(social media plugs in here)*.

- Tactics and activities impacted by social media:
  - real-time, speedy customer response;
  - real-time customer feedback;

- tracking real-time activity;
- troubleshooting;
- sentiment tracking;
- relationship development and nurture tool;
- talent search tool;
- competitor tracking.

HR

- Objectives:

    - increase employee engagement *(social media plugs in here)*;
    - talent management *(social media plugs in here)*.

- Tactics and activities impacted by social media:

    - real-time employee engagement tool;
    - real-time employee feedback;
    - tracking real-time activity;
    - community resource;
    - sentiment tracking;
    - employee development and nurture tool;
    - targeting talent;
    - research.

R&D and product

- Objectives:

    - develop two new product offerings *(social media plugs in here)*;
    - improve user experience *(social media plugs in here)*.

- Tactics and activities impacted by social media:

    - business intelligence;
    - real-time customer feedback;
    - tracking real-time activity;
    - community resource;
    - research.

Given that the point I am illustrating relates to how social media can 'plug in' across the business at both the objective (the what) and tactical level (the how), I purposely have not included any granular KPIs or key results.

Where your personal activity fits in

From that simple illustration, you can see that for you personally there are certain aspects where social media can be 'plugged in' to aspects that have natural 'fit' for you as leader or CEO.

Typically:

- 'What':
  - brand (awareness, reputation);
  - business intelligence (listening, tuning in);
  - customer loyalty (building relationships, loyalty, advocacy);
  - employee engagement (building relationships, loyalty, advocacy);
  - supporting business-wide initiatives (eg launch of a new product).

As part of your personal strategy, we also need to consider the following tactical aspects:

- 'How':
  - which channels you are going to show up on;
  - what is the purpose of each channel;
  - how often you will be visible (frequency and schedule);
  - who (you alone or if you are working with a team);
  - what if... (reputation management, escalation, crisis management, guidelines, processes).

And fundamentally – as leader, some further tactics to consider:

- Personal brand:
  - thought leadership;
  - authenticity;
  - image;
  - content;
  - work–life balance.

Let's work through these areas, providing you with an example of a practical planning matrix to assist in determining your focus and plan.

Determine objectives and then align your social objectives

First things first: as we discussed earlier, to ensure that your social media activity is purposeful and measurable, you want to determine business-wide objectives and then consider how your social activity will dovetail to assist with supporting those objectives.

In this way, what you are setting out to achieve via your social media activity is steered in a very objective way.

Asking the questions:

Your Objective	Your Tactic	Tangible Activities
What do you want to achieve? (Ideally aligned with the organizational objectives.)	How are you going to realize your objective?	What are the desired outcomes that demonstrate your tactics are working?

Let's take a look at a few different examples

The organizational-level objective is to increase brand awareness. Therefore, aligning your objective with that of your organization, so too is your objective.

1 Your objective: increase brand awareness
   Your tactic: what are you going to do?

Sharing expertise via thought leadership activities:

– blogging;
– networking with other thought leaders;
– speaking engagements.

Resulting in:

– more relationships and engagement with and from other thought leaders;
– invitations to speak with other thought leaders;
– invitations to guest blog.

2 Your objective: improve brand reputation
   Your tactic: what are you going to do?

Reputation management:

– amplify internal good news stories;
– set the record straight on any negative PR;
– showcase exemplary examples.

Resulting in:

- increase in positive brand mentions and sentiment;
- reduction in negative sentiment;
- increase in positive engagement.

3 Your objective: improve customer loyalty
Your tactic: what are you going to do?

Tune in and listen to what customers are saying:

- respond and engage directly with customers;
- humanize the brand by showing you care about their viewpoint;
- set the record straight;
- take action to rectify challenges;
- troubleshoot and signpost to resolution;
- be accountable;
- be transparent;
- be authentic.

Resulting in:

- increased positive engagement;
- reduction in negative sentiment;
- increased trust via talking directly with customers;
- reduction in churn;
- increase in upsell and referral (word of mouth), as well as renewal rates;
- increased advocacy generally.

4 Your objective: increase employee engagement
Your tactic: what are you going to do?

Tune in and listen to what employees are saying:

- respond and engage directly with employees;
- humanize your status by showing you care about their viewpoint;
- set the record straight;
- take action to rectify challenges;
- troubleshoot and signpost to resolution;
- be accountable;
- be transparent;
- be authentic.

Resulting in:

– increased employee engagement;
– reduction in negative sentiment;
– increased trust via talking directly with employees;
– increased brand loyalty;
– reduction in employee churn;
– increased advocacy.

5 **Your objective: support two new product launches**
   Your tactic: what are you going to do?

– showcase key benefits and features;
– signpost people to relevant solution and team;
– amplify and advocate promotion.

Resulting in:

– building awareness;
– answering questions or steering to the right source;
– supporting and assisting with the success of the launch.

Once you have determined your social objectives (which align back up to the business-wide objectives), the next stage is to determine which channels you are going to use for which purpose. In Chapter 3 you will recall we explored the social media channels and their typical uses. Whilst it is useful to revisit those uses as you map out your planning process, don't worry too much about flicking back at this stage, as in Chapter 7, where we pull your 90-day plan together, we will be integrating all the components we have discussed so far.

Meanwhile, to assist you with determining your channels, let's explore the following key questions:

'Who are the audience?' and 'which channels are they using?'

If you are looking for engagement, then you need to fish where the fish are and so determining where your audiences are is important.

The demographics and user behaviours we discussed in earlier chapters will help you to determine which social media channels your audiences are likely to favour. Depending on how ingrained social media already is within your organization, it may very well be that audience behaviour, including social media channels, is already part of your business intelligence and management information reporting.

However, that aside, where you personally participate depends on what you are looking to achieve, and what fits better for you as a leader. For example, it may be that from an organizational perspective, or product offering, your audience falls in the age group 15–20. Therefore, they are highly likely to be active on Snapchat and Instagram. However, if your personal objective is focusing on the more B2B aspects, developing corporate partnerships or investor relationships, then as leader or CEO your activity may focus around thought leadership, using LinkedIn and Twitter.

It may be that you leave your social media team to focus on the day-to-day direct customer engagement, whilst you focus your attention in other areas. You are still publicly out there, but from a more business development, partnership positioning than from the perspective of directly talking to customers.

When you look at Chapter 8 and some of the examples from other CEOs and leaders, you will see that, from an output perspective, things vary. John Legere from T-Mobile has direct conversations with employees and customers. Brian Dunn from Best Buy mentions the importance of talking to and listening in to customers and employees, whilst Kevin Burrowes from PwC focuses more on the thought leadership aspect.

What you do is driven by what you want to achieve. Put simply, strategy dictates tactics. This illustrates the importance of mapping out what your objectives are and how you are going to focus your attention:

- the audiences you target;
- the channels you use;
- the content you create;
- the outcomes you measure.

Plan, but don't lose the human touch

From a planning perspective, as with most things in life you want to find some balance. You want to find a balance between planning to be objectively driven so that your activity is purposeful and supports the wider business objectives, and having the freedom to share views and content in an organic, human and natural way.

The essence of social media is fundamentally being 'social' and, if you liken it to being physically social, and think about conversations, then being objectively driven with every conversation you have would very quickly become fairly dull. However, also be mindful that there are some conversations where there has been a lot of preparation prior to having them, let's say for example in a planned meeting.

Not sure of how to strike this balance? Well, that leads me very nicely into the value of listening.

Listen

In my view, listening is far more important than engaging. When consulting or training, I like to pop up a slide of the human face to drive home the point.

Two eyes, two ears and just one mouth, so let's use them in accordance.

In fact, as we uncovered earlier in Chapter 2, many people 'tune in' on social media without ever engaging. Again, without exception, the leaders interviewed in Chapter 8 each highlight the value of tuning in and listening in real time.

Listening on social media can be very 'scientific'. There are a number of sophisticated tools geared to track sentiment, engagement and other facets, providing organizations with useful business intelligence.

However, taking a hands-on pragmatic and simplistic approach can be just as insightful. Getting out into the channels and running some basic searches to get a feel for what's going on in the space gives you enough of a feel for sentiment. It's not statistically significant but, as Brian Dunn, former CEO of Best Buy, told me in his interview:

> Getting real-time feedback on public opinion… not statistically accurate but typically directionally accurate. A great way to take the consumers'

temperature on any given topic relating to your business and an interesting data point on your competitors.

Let's explore what you as leader can be tuning in to, and then some quick ways to stay tuned via your mobile, without the need for complex technology.

Tuning in...

When it comes to what you can be listening for and tuning in to, there are a number of areas that may be useful:

- **Customers**

  What they are saying, how they are feeling, or the overall sentiment they have about your organization.

- **Competitors**

  What they are up to, what people are saying about them, and how they, in turn, are engaging with people.

- **Partners**

  What is happening in their world and how that relates back to your organization.

- **Suppliers**

  What is happening in their world and how that relates back to your organization.

- **Influencers or thought leaders**

  What they are talking about: what the hot topics are that the industry is debating.

- **Investors**

  What is happening in their world and how that relates back to your organization.

When it comes to helping you to get clarity on the content you share, or how you are going to engage, just from that short list above, I'm sure that already you are building a picture of how you could be engaging. Hopefully, it triggered a bit of an 'aha' moment for you, and if it didn't then don't worry, as we will talk more in just a while about the practicalities of engaging.

Of course, it is not just about tuning in to what is going on outside your organization; there is a lot to be gleaned by tuning inwards too:

- **Employees**

   What are the charitable activities the team is involved with? Are there new hires, awards, efforts or wins? What is happening in the world of your organization and via your employees?

- **Thought leaders**

   Who are the socially savvy executives, leaders, champions, influencers, bloggers and high social media users within your company?

Then, of course, there's the macro environment: general, topical news stories, trending topics, events and seasonal activities.

Focused listening rather than unfocused publishing

My advice is not to overthink 'listening' but rather just to start listening. It will uncover many things that provide useful hooks for you to hang your activity around.

It is far better to be answering questions or being part of a relevant conversation rather than simply pushing out content that doesn't chime with your audience. It's far better to respond to need than guess what you think is going to be useful. For example, if you see a number of customers all asking the same question, or complaining about the same issue, this presents the perfect recipe for an effective and engaging response or content development.

Similarly, it may be that another influencer or thought leader has posted a viewpoint about a topic that you have some views about. Whether you agree or disagree, you can jump into that conversation, either commenting or sharing and, where relevant, adding your own viewpoint.

I often get asked about where to source content, or how to know what to talk about on social media. My retort is always the same: if you've got opinions about something and you are passionate about what you do, and you care about your employees and customers, then by simply tuning in you will find all the fuel you need.

Quick ways to tune in

From a 'listening' perspective, understanding how your organization is currently monitoring the social media channels and tuning in to relevant audiences is a good place to start. You may already have some insights to guide your activity, and such data may be built into your management information reports.

Given that social media is so 'real time' you may also want to 'listen in' to things quickly via your smartphone. Here are a few ways you can quickly tune in.

Search the networks

By far the simplest and quickest way to figure out what is going on in real time on each of the social media networks is by running some quick searches in their search box. Each of the social media networks has a search box. Simply typing in your brand name, company name, @tag or hashtag into the search box will return real-time results.

Google alerts

Basic alert but it's amazing how many good insights I still pick up from Google alerts. You can track alerts to be sent directly to your email address on pretty much anything – brand name, your name, company name, competitors. You can set when they arrive, in real time or once a day, or once a week. It is free to use and super simple to set up alerts.

Track your organization's social media accounts

What better way to see how people are responding to the content your organization is sharing than to tune in to your organization's corporate social media accounts? I'm always stunned by just how many leaders and CEOs are not tuned in to what is being shared by their own organizations. Simply follow your own accounts on social media to stay tuned. You can share, retweet and respond, amplifying organizational news to your audiences – and of course, where relevant, they can share your activity too.

Listening generally comes *before* engaging. Listen, observe and learn. Don't underestimate just how much you can learn about being effective by simply tuning in and seeing what works for others. This works in the offline world too!

Analyse

When it comes to analysis, we are in the age of data overload and, with social media, there is so much data to consider.

As stated earlier, you may have tools undertaking deeper analysis and providing you and your organization with insights and business intelligence. However, keeping things simple and from a practical perspective, you have listened and tuned in and heard and learnt a few things. Therefore, this 'analyse' aspect is really about digesting that learning and figuring out 'what' you are going to do about it.

Simple observational analysis around who, what, when and where:

- Who's saying what?
- How active are certain people?
- What themes regularly come up?
- Who is engaging and what is their demographic profile?
- Are you noticing any patterns?
- Are there any key influencers who regularly engage and share your content? Who are they and what can you be doing, if anything, to engage further?
- What is getting engagement, what is chiming with your audiences?
- What are people engaging with from a media perspective? Does video seem to be the zeitgeist and, if so, is it long- or short-form video? Or perhaps it's quotes or memes or images?
- When are people engaging? Have you noticed whether there is an optimum time of day or day of the week?
- What do conversations look like on each channel and how do they differ?

The key is to remember that the purpose for this observational analysis is to assist you with uncovering how you do things better and to help steer your activity.

Engage

As we looked at in more detail earlier in the book, communications have changed. Therefore, for you as a leader, communication competencies have changed. Keeping pace with changes calls for an expanded skill base. Communications are far less corporate and far more human.

Trust is everything. Authentic conversations and transparency matter.

You're clear on objectives, you've done the listening and analysis – so you're au fait with your landscape. Now it's down to the practicalities of getting out there and engaging.

As mentioned earlier, whilst having a plan and being objectively driven is important, social media is a highly organic and conversational beast. If your activity looks too programmatic and not authentically driven, that will most certainly translate.

As a leader or CEO, you are heavily invested in your organization or brand. Your purpose is protector, educator, champion and evangelist. You are also a person with your own values, interests and views. This gives you a rich and varied remit for your social media activity.

Passionate about the role of social media in leadership, I'm always tuned in to what some of the 'social leaders' are up to. To illustrate the point about the importance of having rich and varied content, over the past couple of days, Stephen Kelly, CEO of Sage Group plc, has shared the following types of tweets on Twitter:

- A curated article on AI and its impact on business. This is a thought leadership piece that clearly fits in with the audience Sage serves.

- A curated article on entrepreneurs and the importance of collaboration. This, again, is a thought leadership piece that is relevant to his audience.

- A restaurant recommendation, which is something more personal and works in making him appear more genuine and authentic, a regular person.

- A congratulatory message to team members on a recent software innovation award, which directly aids his employee engagement efforts as a CEO.

- A retweet of a post from a Sage event taking place in Canada, which a Sage team member had posted, thus again signifying to his employees that he is present and cares, further enhancing his employee engagement efforts.

- A general topical post, sending 'Happy Diwali' wishes to colleagues, partners and customers, which aids in humanizing his Twitter profile by sharing something personal.

There are a multitude of uses of social media that well-known CEOs have been exploiting. Uber's CEO, Dara Khosrowshahi, for example, has been an active face of the company as it is going through difficult times, purposefully engaging with his drivers and customers. A LinkedIn influencer and avid Twitter user, Khosrowshahi has recently been praising his team and drivers for their patience and generally keeping all those tuned in up to speed with developments in the current battle for Uber to keep its licence in London. He is using social media in a way that fosters a transparent, authentic and genuine dialogue.

Others, like Lloyd Blankfein from Goldman Sachs and John Legere from T-Mobile, use social media to communicate specific information about their companies to the press and relevant stakeholders. Blankfein, for example, routinely tweets content that would have traditionally been released to the press via press releases, taking the view that since most journalists are on Twitter, it makes sense to engage with them through that medium. Legere, on the other hand, shares T-Mobile's quarterly results on Twitter, Instagram and Periscope, though that is not to say he couldn't do so on internal platforms as well for his employees.

Best practice when engaging

How you engage and what you engage with tends to fall into place once you get started. The more you practise, the more you will get into your flow. Because being 'social' is such a human and authentic activity, you will need to find your own way. But here are some aspects to consider when getting started:

- Whilst you are the leader or CEO, don't come from a position of knowing everything, but rather, always be curious. Ask open questions and seek opinion from your audiences. Such openness has shown to drive engagement.

- Be honest and gracious. If you have listened and learnt something about challenges that can help shape your future business, acknowledge it and say thank you.

- Don't be afraid to be honest about the challenges you are facing. Showing vulnerability is authentic and honest. Authenticity and honesty build trust.

- Give, give, give. Focus on helping rather than taking.

- Put your efforts where your audiences are and where you want to build and engage a community.

- Be a great social media leader. Bring your leadership stance to the social media table. Produce relevant and purposeful content that challenges, provokes and ignites your audiences.

- Connect and engage with other leaders, thought leaders and key influencers. Create connections that create conversation.

- Be authentic. Being engaged on social media is inherently 'being social'. You can't fake it. Own it and make it yours.

How to strike a work and personal balance

Striking the work and personal view balance is a matter for personal reflection. It really comes back to determining your purpose and aligning with business-wide objectives.

In my interview with Dr Sam Collins she suggests that as leaders we should all be a little 'bolder'. She refers to the Campbell's Soup campaign in the summer of 2017, and the stance taken by the organization responding to homophobic negative sentiment received in light of their 'two dads' advertising campaign. Campbell's Soup stood their ground, but did so eloquently, with both wit and graciousness. Whilst their stance clearly upset those who were outraged by the campaign, their courage to publicly stand their ground sparked sincere and heartfelt respect for the brand. It engendered positive share of mind for the brand, which otherwise would not have had opportunity to manifest itself.

Being controversial can unite or backfire and as leader or CEO you are the lead brand champion, the brand protector. The stance you take will depend on your role within the organization, the strategic positioning of your personal brand, the brand values, your values and your objectives.

The hardest part of engaging authentically is just doing it. As I said earlier, there is no better way to get started than to get started. But getting out of your own way is a challenge. Let's not underestimate the impact of fear and vulnerability in preventing leaders from sharing their knowledge.

Remember, back in the Introduction, I mentioned my why for writing this book, and the fact that I have coached leaders, totally anonymously, because they do not want anyone to know that they are not 100 per cent up to speed on social media. That's a true story.

The higher your position, the more pressure and paranoia around getting things wrong, making mistakes and losing credibility. However, being human, honest and transparent is often the best retort on social media. If you don't have the answer, then that's okay, you just openly say that you don't know but you will check it out with someone who does and either you or someone that does know will get back to them.

It seems simple enough, but for some of us, this conversational way of 'being social' is more of a mindset shift, and it takes practice. The fear of getting it wrong is very real. It may be that English is not your first language and you are concerned about grammar or typos and losing credibility.

I'm sure we all remember a time when a communication has been taken the wrong way, perhaps an email taken out of context. Well those same concerns are at play when we are on social media.

In one respect, everything moves so fluidly on social media. However, being prepared, lining up contingency plans and crisis management tactics just in case anything 'escalates', is all part of good planning.

As Caron Bradshaw, CEO of Charity Finance Group (CFG) says:

I perceive that social media is as much about the 'social' as it is about the 'media', thus I am not afraid to show myself. That is not to say that I will talk about anything and everything – there are limits to what I feel would be appropriate to share (and topics where CFG have deliberately not taken a stance where it would be unhelpful to comment or engage too heavily). The relationships that you can form from social media connections are important and it is unlikely that a cold, broadcasting or dictating approach would engage with people who I have not met, and may never meet. It would also not be the authentic me. I like to chat, I have a creative mind and I feel relationships are so important. By showing myself authentically, I hope that this reinforces what CFG is striving to be. I hope it strengthens our brand and promotes a positive image of CFG.

A lot of people I've spoken to (particularly those who are not big social media users) are scared about the risks associated with putting out content that hasn't gone through a rigorous process and scrutiny. I see it more as an extension to less formal communications that you might have, say, at a networking event. You use judgement on what to share and what not to say, you engage in positive conversations and walk away from those that are going nowhere – and you definitely don't hit the wine! Of course, when you put something out there in writing it does have a greater level of permanence. I don't tend to worry too much about silly typos or getting something wrong innocently. It's easy to laugh at your own typos or to correct misunderstandings provided that you are not reckless. On the other side, it is too easy to allow social media to take over without it being a valuable or meaningful addition to your work, so I would caution people about spending too much time trying to respond to everything. I think that the balance in what you say is important; too much 'here is what my work is doing' can feel like a salesperson touting for business (not in itself a bad thing but I don't think helpful to a CEO); conversely, too much personal stuff or opinion can narrow your network rather than expand it. Finally, I would encourage people to show up – to be themselves and give it a go. Don't let someone else do it for you (people will see through it); try a little at first and see where it takes you. It's not about the volume of followers you have (though clearly the broader the network the greater the potential pool of people to engage with), it's more about the quality of the conversations that your social media presence can lead to.

In the above excerpt from her interview, Caron raises two key points around the same theme. Both points relate to being mindful and conscious about the risks when communicating via social media, and the permanence of digital communications. Just because a tweet gets deleted, it doesn't disappear from the digital landscape. It could already have been screen-grabbed and shared.

Whilst throughout this book there is a theme of authenticity and transparency, so too is there a theme of leadership and responsibility to your organization, your audience and yourself. Largely, it is about best judgement. If it doesn't feel right to share or say something publicly, then best to err on the side of caution. If you do decide to take a stand on something, then do so in a considered and potentially concerted way. Weigh up the potential responses and speak with your internal communication teams regarding policy and positioning.

No man is an island

When pulling your plan together, pull in all the relevant resources you can. If there is already a social media team on board looking after the organizational social media activities, then it's wise to tune in to what they are doing, how they are doing their planning, and how they see your personal activity fitting in.

Whilst I, and indeed all those interviewed, advise that the best person to be doing your personal social media activity is you, there are indeed aspects that you can get assistance with:

- Content creation: this may include video and creative images sourced, help with writing thought leadership pieces, or general language, grammar or translations, and sense checks.

- Listening and tuning in: though some of this can be automated for you too via social media listening dashboards such as Hootsuite, Sprout Social and Buffer (as mentioned in Chapter 3), which you can use via apps on your mobile.

- Data and insights: if your organization already has business intelligence reports around your typical audience demographics and their social media activity, and which channels they are on, then you have already got some great insight as to which channels serve you best for reaching those audiences.

- Channel set-up and optimization: whilst those who have developed the social channels have made them intuitive to set up, you can still use your internal social media team, if relevant, or marketing or comms teams, to assist you with ensuring your social platforms are set up appropriately. They will be able to assist with branding and images and ensure any links to corporate accounts and relevant hashtags are on board. I have provided you with some pointers too to assist with profile optimization in Chapter 3 – and you will find more specific step-by-step set-up guides on the www.getsocial.site, should you need them.

- Training: let's take a look at this in more detail below.

Social media training

In a previous role, prior to being let loose to discuss what our organization was up to with the press, I was given formal 'media training'. In your role as 'leader', it is highly likely that you too may have embarked upon such training. It is fairly standard to ensure that 'spokespersons' for an organization have encountered some relevant training.

Hence why, for exactly the same reasons, it is important that you understand exactly how social media channels work and you get some training prior to engaging. As mentioned earlier on, social media training for C-suite and leadership teams is fast becoming business as usual.

As Kevin Burrowes mentions in his interview, there are two strands of training within PwC: social media masterclasses and e-learning, providing practical training around the channel options and best practice; and then also a reverse mentoring programme, where partners and directors spend time with junior members of staff to learn about how to best deploy social media and channels to build their personal brand and connect with clients and stakeholders. Lego has also introduced social media exams for their leadership team. As social media has moved beyond the marketing team, so too has the training competence across organizations.

If you haven't had any training on social media, then I encourage you to do so. This may take the form of spending some lunchtime sessions with your in-house social media team, or embarking on a one-to-one coaching session or, perhaps, you too may champion social media exams happening within your C-suite.

For example, if you send out a message and you need to retract it or edit it – what do you do? For each of the platforms, it differs slightly. Getting comfortable with how each one operates – or at least the ones you are going to be using – will give you immense comfort that you are in control.

We will explore further in Chapter 7, in your 90-day plan, a few of the aspects that, as a social media practitioner, you want to be completely up to speed with for day-to-day activity.

Measure

It is fair to say that there is probably more data readily accessible to us than at any other point in time. Big data is big business.

The marketer in me is a huge advocate for data-driven activity, as how will we ever know what is working and how to optimize and iterate, if we don't measure effectiveness?

However, with social media, given there is so much data realized, it is important to take a step back and ensure that what you are measuring actually matters. From a very basic perspective for me, zoning in on the 'little data' with laser focus is about getting down to the nitty gritty of measuring what really matters.

In just the same way that your social media activity is objectively driven, then the real measure will be whether your activity helped you to deliver these objectives or not. If you don't start with the end in mind, how will you ever know if you got there?

Let's take a quick look at purpose and measures:

When you first start out on social, you will need to grow your base, likes and followers. We will explore the practicalities of growing a targeted and relevant following in Chapter 7, when pulling together your 90-day plan. Therefore, the number of followers you have on each account will be a gauge of you want to measure:

Network	Followers Week 1	Followers Week 2	Followers Week 3	Followers Week 4
Twitter	50	150	200	250
LinkedIn	500	700	900	1000
Instagram	50	90	150	220

Other data that will be useful in helping you to steer your activity will focus around engagement: sharing, retweeting, commenting or liking. What got the most retweets, shares, likes, comments?

Engagement metrics are really useful in helping you to determine what chimes with your audience and understand which messaging and positioning is favoured on different channels. They can greatly assist with your content development.

Other metrics to consider are those where you are asking your audience to do something with particular call-to-action aspects such as get involved, sign up, take a poll. These I refer to as 'action metrics'. Again, depending on what you are setting out to achieve, these may form part of the metrics you want to measure:

Engagement Metrics	Growth Metrics	Action Metrics
• Likes • Shares • Comments • Retweets	• Consistently growing your baseline	Did the message provoke the necessary call to action? • Download • Renewal • Survey or poll • Promo link • Sign up

When developing a simple set of key metrics that help you identify whether the activities you are undertaking are actually delivering against your objectives, consider the following questions:

- What does success look like? What objectives or desired outcomes are you trying to achieve?
- What metrics and evidence do I need so that I can measure that success or progress?
- How am I going to get this data to ensure I am continuously capturing, monitoring and learning from my activity?

The 'how' of how you collect and collate data is an important question to figure out. Again, this is something that as leader or CEO you can get help with from those in your team already doing social media, or via your data team. Failing that, it is about creating a schedule and mapping it each week, month or quarter.

Measuring what matters and ROI

For you as leader or CEO, it is likely your focus will be on brand, reputation, thought leadership and customer and employee engagement.

You're busy, and so you will be keen to know that your activity is bringing some results. The challenge with social media and with many aspects of 'brand' activity is that some of the impact is not so tangible and, therefore, measurable.

Sure, you can track growth, actions and engagement. But there are a lot of people who passively engage, and that's just something you cannot directly capture.

I love the question asked by social media and digital thought leader Gary Vaynerchuk when referring to social media ROI – he asks: 'What's the ROI of your mother?'

In a post by Gary on LinkedIn Pulse, he explains that whilst largely there is a lot of data to be gleaned from social media channels, the real ROI depends on what you do with it, how engaged you are, the content you share, the message you create and the impact you make (Vaynerchuk, 2015). In the same post, he poses the question, what's the ROI of a piano? For him, approximately £26.50; for Elton John, $400 million. The key point he makes around ROI is that there is not a one-size-fits-all ROI calculation and the return goes beyond the data that you can physically get your hands on.

However, whilst the main impact may be difficult to calculate, there are a number of aspects that can be captured, aspects you can map into, measuring your activity as CEO or leader:

- Increase brand awareness:
  - Are you growing *relevant* followers?

- Establish credibility and trust:
  - Are you getting endorsements/shares from *influential* people?
  - How is your audience responding to these influencers?
  - Are those influencers extending the reach of your audience?

- Connect with your audience:
  - Is your audience responding well to your content?
  - Is the content you share encouraging *engagement*?
  - What levels of shares, reach and discussion is your content achieving?

- Find new leads/drive sales:
  - Is social activity bringing people back to your website/landing page?
  - Have you achieved a certain amount of sign-ups/downloads?
  - How is social helping you to retain/engage customers/employees?

The above questions are by no means the only questions you need to be considering. However, they provide you with a good starting point to get the ROI conversation started.

As you embark on the world of social media, finding return on your investment is possible, particularly if you have set very clear objectives. Therefore, start with the end in mind: plan, listen, analyse, engage and measure.

Remember these three things

1 Set goals that align with the whole business rather than just social. Remember, those that aim for nothing, hit it with remarkable accuracy.

2 Being social or getting social whilst at first may be something you intentionally 'do' – fundamentally, you want it to become something you 'are' – an extension of you and your everyday role.

3 Being social is fundamentally about being 'social'. The more human and authentic your activity, the more trustworthy and engaging.

Take action

As part of your 90-day plan in Chapter 7, we will focus on each of these key aspects:

- Align your activity with that of your organization. Review what is going on already within your organization around social – how it is working, who is involved, what the contingency plans are, what the guidelines are, what they are measuring – and understand how your activity fits in.

- Tune in and actively listen to what is happening in the space. Run simple searches and work with your social media team so that you are up to date with insights that may already have been gleaned.

- Measure what matters. Develop a measurement effectiveness matrix that works for you. Deliver on the objectives that you are setting out to achieve.

- Get some social media training and skill up. It may be useful to find a friendly internal or external 'mentor' who you can work with for a few weeks until you are fully up to speed, answering questions and checking over how you are doing. You will be far better equipped if you are more informed on how the channels work and how you can easily share updates and engage. Before you know it, it will become business as usual.

Reference

Vaynerchuk, Gary (2015) [accessed 29 November 2017] What's the ROI of Your Mother?, *LinkedIn Pulse*, 13 November [Online] https://www.linkedin.com/pulse/whats-roi-your-mother-gary-vaynerchuk

06
The social business

In the previous chapter, we focused on your personal social media strategy, largely focusing on the 'external' use of social media.

To frame this, let's look at the following model. There are internal and external audiences and internal and external uses for social media:

Internally facing (You)	Externally facing (You)
Your personal social media activity with your internal colleagues and operations, which may include employees, internal influencers and thought leaders. 1	Your personal social media activity with your external audiences, which may include customers, partners, influencers and thought leaders. 2
Internally facing (Your organization)	**Externally facing (Your organization)**
Your organization's social media activity operationally and with internal colleagues. 3	Your organization's social media activity with external audiences, which may include customers, influencers, partners and thought leaders. 4

Much of what we discussed in Chapter 5 focused on quadrants 1 and 2, your personal activity within and beyond your organization.

Of course, the other dynamic to consider is what is happening with social media across your organization. How is social media being utilized operationally within the organization to facilitate collaboration, shared knowledge and improved communications? How is your organization engaging from a social media perspective with external audiences?

In this chapter, we will touch on both these aspects, briefly exploring organizational social media strategy, looking at the ways that social media can be utilized, and the implications for you as leader.

It may be that as a leader, organizational strategy is something you direct, steer, contribute towards, or it is a key function of one of your colleagues in the 'C-suite', perhaps a chief digital officer. Or perhaps none of the above, and it is something you are eager to develop.

Back in Chapter 3, I invited you to 'stop calling it social media', and instead refer to it as 'a highly connected, highly democratized communications vehicle'. From an organizational perspective, social media technologies and social media present opportunities for teams to work collaboratively, regardless of location. It is an important component of digital transformation.

More instantaneous connection, more collaboration, speedier access to knowledge and centralization are all available to those organizations and leaders that are keen to embrace it.

What you will learn from this chapter

- Exploring how social media fits in across your organization.
- How it can map into current technologies.
- Some frameworks and benchmarks so that you can 'test' how your organization measures up.

As a leader, when considering where social media fits with you, there are a few areas that naturally 'fit', namely, brand, reputation, customer engagement and employee engagement. From an organizational perspective, each of these areas can also be significantly impacted by social media. You should also add to these operational effectiveness and internal communications, as these are two other areas where social media has the opportunity to make direct impact.

As a leader or CEO considering embarking upon social media activity, are you clear on the following:

- How is social media being used across the organization?
- How is social media managed within the organization: is it managed in-house or by an agency?
- In which department or team does it currently reside?
- Does social media activity align with internal communication technologies; for example, are you using internal social media networks?
- Does social media plug in to your customer relationship management (CRM) system so that you can see the real-time updates from colleagues, partners, customers?
- Is leadership integrated with social media? Are members of your C-suite already participating?
- Is there a company-wide social media training policy?
- Are there company-wide social media guidelines in place and readily accessible for all employees?
- How are the team assessed for their social media competencies and activity?

How is social media organized across your organization?

In Chapter 5 we looked at how social media has the potential to plug in to each of the different business units to assist with delivering against objectives, as demonstrated in Figure 6.1.

Figure 6.1 Plugging in social media to meet business objectives

Organizational social media – external facing

As outlined in the quadrant at the beginning of this chapter, there are a number of layers to consider with regards to where social media sits and how it will be leveraged within an organization.

Let's first start with the 'external facing' aspect. First, it is useful to determine where social media resides and how it is controlled within the organization. For your organization's external-facing social media communications, is there a 'central' social media team that is responsible for brand reputation, customer engagement, product and service promotion, and marketing activity across the entire business? This is outlined in Figure 6.2.

Centralization can be useful as it brings a certain consistency of communications and messaging. Campaigns, tone of voice, and analysis and data capture can be optimized as everything is in one place. On the downside, centralization can stifle programmes, particularly if it becomes too bureaucratic and process-focused. Speed of response and authentic human communication and engagement are expected on social media. Therefore, the importance of this 'agile' aspect should not be underestimated.

Figure 6.2 Social media that is centrally managed

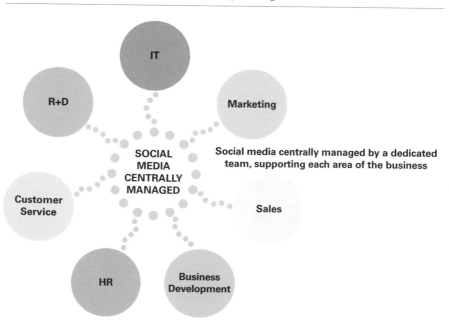

Or is it the case that one, two or a few divisions, usually marketing, HR, sales and business development, have already made headway and have started with social media activity, without there ever being a formal 'central' process in place? Teams may have proceeded to develop accounts, practices, audiences and messaging that specifically fit their objectives, giving each division responsibility for their own external social media activity. This is illustrated in Figure 6.3.

If you are an organization with a number of brands and products that each have their own marketing, sales, R&D, customer service and business development teams, then you are more likely to be working with a dispersed model as illustrated in Figure 6.3.

I've seen cases where this has worked out successfully, with learning and knowledge from those teams empowered to get to grips with social media being shared and transferred into other areas of the business, thus facilitating shared learning and developing best practice. Conversely, I've also seen cases where divisions and teams have been keen to embrace social media, and have done so without any central guidance. This resulted in brand and tone of voice not necessarily being on message.

Figure 6.3 Each department, brand or product has their own social media activity

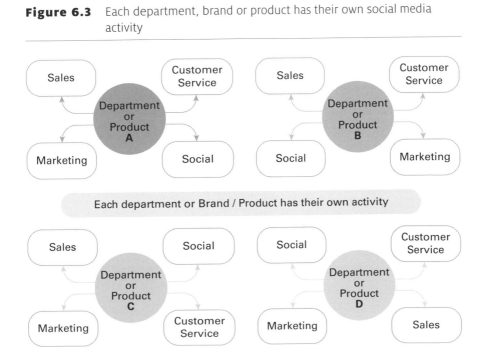

The other challenge, of course, is that once activity has got started and teams are enthusiastic about what they are doing, and in some cases are seeing great results, trying to rein in such practices to align with brand and overall objectives can become a little like herding cats.

When it comes to organizational social media strategy and tactics, there is no one-size-fits-all methodology. The type of business you are, your infrastructure and, importantly, your culture, will determine the best approach.

You may have a centralized model, or a dispersed local model – or indeed it may be that you operate a hybrid. Each division, brand or product may have their own 'social' team that works with a central social team, keeping brand and tone of voice in line, sharing knowledge, learning and competence, yet still retaining the agile, local brand or business unit engagement. This is illustrated in Figure 6.4.

As I said earlier, any model you adopt has to work for you. However, deciding on structure and mapping who the team is and how social media can be integrated is now a key part of strategic endeavour.

Figure 6.4   Central social media team supporting individual social media teams

Each Product or Department has autonomy, but there is a Central Social Team supporting and aligning the individual Social Teams.

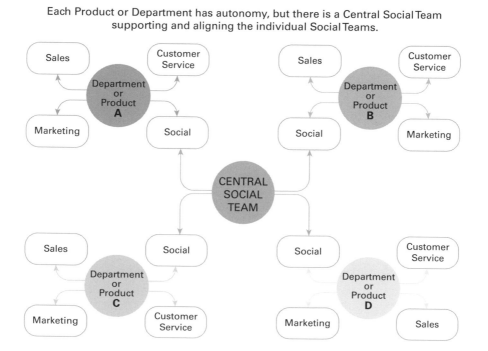

Organizational social media – internal facing

Let's now turn to look at the internal-facing aspects of social media from an organizational perspective.

Given the adoption heritage of social media within organizations, mainly focused on using the channel for 'marketing and broadcast' purposes, then it is no surprise that initially social media was largely an externally focused activity.

As the years have passed and social media has been embraced and integrated more widely across organizations, social media and social media technologies and the boundary-less engagement, the sharing of ideas, the one-to-one and one-to-many real-time conversations they enable with external audiences have been realized as key communication and collaboration resources across organizations for internal audiences. Businesses are now tapping into their potential for assisting with internal communications, internal collaboration, shared knowledge, data integration, project management and remote and flexible working processes.

A great example is Workplace by Facebook, which is Facebook's enterprise solution, enabling organizations to leverage all the benefits of Facebook for teams. Rather than people having to learn how to leverage new social technologies, Workplace provides an enterprise solution of a platform that over 3 billion people are already familiar with.

Heineken, for example, uses Facebook's Workplace for internal collaboration: 'It's very intuitive and people are already very familiar with how to use Facebook. No special instructions required' (Miller, 2013). Royal Bank of Scotland also encourages employees to use Facebook at work: 'Facebook Workplace lets our staff communicate, discuss and solve problems faster and more efficiently in a way that tools, such as email, simply can't' (Miller, 2013).

These two examples are taken from Rachel Miller's evergreen blog post, 'Who's Using What for Internal Social Media?', showcasing over 400 user cases, started in 2013 and continuously updated. Rachel has curated case studies from organizations across the world, looking at uses of resources such as Facebook's Workplace, Slack, Google Apps, Jive, Snapcoms, Sharepoint, Chatter, Social Cast, Social Text and Yammer.

Some organizations have created bespoke internal social media systems and technologies to optimize collaboration and shared knowledge. Others have taken advantage of the enterprise solutions that the traditional social media channels have evolved or, as seen below, are perhaps managing a balance of both.

Managing a balance of both enterprise and native mainstream social media tools may not be intentional. As mentioned in the Heineken case study, those using Workplace were already comfortable with Facebook; there were no new systems to learn about, but rather, the enablement of familiar systems deployed to people and teams for work purposes.

The reality is that if you give people the right tools and permissions, they will collaborate. If you make it difficult for them to collaborate by giving them tools that make being social and collaborative difficult, or there are constraints that don't enable communication in the way it needs to happen, then they either will not use them effectively, or they will simply adopt their own 'desire line' and make their own path.

Therefore, understanding which tools your employees are currently familiar with, and what they enjoy about them as platforms, can – and in my view should – become part of the discussion and initial research and fact finding around organizational adoption of internal social technologies.

Enterprise resources such as CRM have become totally conversant with social media technologies, enabling organizations to fully optimize knowledge and insight in a real-time perspective.

This, again, works two ways. Whilst it is useful that organizations can pull in real-time data on individuals, contacts and organizations, such enterprise solutions will be realizing the same advantages for the executives they are looking to connect with.

To reference Kevin Burrowes's interview:

When I have business meetings, especially with someone I've never met before, I often look at Google and Salesforce to find out more about that person. Social media profiles come up top of the search every time. For this reason alone it is so important to make sure your profiles are up to date. It could be a bad first impression if not! Having an out-of-date LinkedIn profile or empty Twitter feed really doesn't look good.

Leaders who don't engage with social risk being left behind. Social media is just a way of life for many millennials who are moving into more and more senior management positions. We've got to keep up!

To support Kevin's point around social being a way of life for those moving into more senior management positions, a recent Holmes Noble report, 'The DNA of a Modern CEO', cites that by 2030 millennials will be approximately 75 per cent of the global workforce (Holmes Noble, 2017), and that millennials are changing the workforce and are quickly rising up the leadership ranks. (You will recall that in Chapter 2 we uncovered the statistics and data around millennial social media adoption.)

Such social technology literacy can create advantages for organizations looking to embrace new ways of working. The challenge, however, as discussed in the brilliant book by Rob Goffee and Gareth Jones, *Why Should Anyone Work Here? What it takes to create an authentic organization*, is for organizations to master the tricky balance of allowing employees to be themselves in order to get the best out of them, without imposing too many constraining rules (Goffee and Jones, 2015).

Social media guidelines are now a staple within the majority of organizations, but if they are presented in a 78-page, bureaucratic white paper format, more akin to a complex, jargon-laden contract, rather than useful practical guidelines, then realistically, how simple are they for employees to engage with and, importantly, to adhere to?

I love the position that Goffee and Jones take in their 'simplifying the rules' chapter, asking leaders to be aware of 'rule creep'. They pose the question that when something goes wrong, is creating another rule the best outcome?

Those two key points around technologies that are familiar and, therefore, friction free and getting the balance of freedom and responsibility in how employees communicate, raise significant issues for social media adoption within organizations – and it's the same ones we explored in Chapter 5. Social media is not purely about technology. The technology is the enabler. The 'connect anywhere, 24/7' aspect that the cloud enables is important; the data that is gleaned and the analytics can be highly informative; the simplicity of the user interface to invite natural adoption and engender connection, reach and engagement – these are all important factors of the technology.

However, the bigger issue really drives back to having a 'socially literate' culture. A culture that teaches, embeds, nurtures and facilitates collaboration, co-creation, conversation, engagement and the sharing of knowledge.

The technology will facilitate insights, but it is not just what the tools can provide for you, but also what you are communicating to and for others, internally and externally. Social media technologies in business are clearly becoming more commonplace and proving themselves to deliver effective and cost-efficient ways of working for organizations.

A 10-year research programme (2005–15) by McKinsey & Co, 'Evolution of Social Technologies', surveyed in excess of 2,700 global executives around social media technology adoption: 45 per cent say social media technologies are now very integrated into day-to-day work (Harrysson, Schoder and Tavakoli, 2016).

Key benefits cited were:

- greater access to knowledge and to experts within and outside the enterprise;
- cost reductions due to more effective internal communications, eg video-sharing platforms to engage with customers remotely rather than travelling;
- engaging the workforce to actively advocate brand/business on social and contribute by helping your customers in any way possible.

Most interestingly, their paper highlights another degree of collaboration, relating to companies setting strategic priorities from the bottom up, through involving employees through social voting mechanisms: 47 per cent of companies in their survey stated that such democratization of strategy 'would intensify over the next three to five years' (Harrysson, Schoder and Tavakoli, 2016).

Capgemini Consulting, in association with MIT Sloan Management, have also published a report: 'The Digital Advantage: How digital leaders outperform their peers in every industry'. Their report offers insight into research undertaken over two years, with over 450 senior executives in 391 large companies around the world.

The research focused on uncovering and measuring 'digital maturity' across sectors to determine the impact on financial performance and competitive advantage and to uncover any specific patterns and common linkages between domains of excellence.

The research charts four types of digital maturity:

- **Digirati:** truly understand how to drive value with digital transformation.
- **Fashionistas:** implement or experiment with many digital applications.
- **Beginners:** do very little with advanced digital capabilities.
- **Conservatives:** favour prudence over innovation.

The research examines six digital intensity domains:

1 customer experience;

2 social media;

3 mobile;

4 customer analytics;

5 process digitization;

6 internal collaboration (using internal social media resources).

Their findings uncover that when looking at revenue generation, profitability and market valuation, companies that fall into the Digirati segment outperform all other categories to a greater or lesser degree. The companies that fell within the Digirati category encompassed sectors that included banking, retail and high-tech. These were all sectors where social media is being optimized to engage the mobile, social customer, whilst also facilitating internal knowledge sharing.

The research identified a Digirati model that offers clear patterns of advantage. These included leveraging customer-facing processes, including social media, customer experience and mobile, and integrating with operational processes, analytics, process digitization and internal collaboration, particularly with the use of internal social networks.

Whilst social media is not in and of itself 'digital transformation' it is certainly recognized as a key component, and how 'social media' impacts competitive advantage is a hot topic of research. The Center for the Future of Organization at the Peter Drucker School of Management has developed an index that measures the capability of leaders and their organizations to 'Leverage Social Media for Competitive Advantage'.

Whilst the OSML Index® – Organizational Social Media Literacy – specifically targets senior leaders in larger organizations with complex layers of hierarchy and management, the questions posed within that survey provide anyone with a useful framework for uncovering their social media baseline and asks relevant questions that invite deeper thought and analysis.

The OSML Index® is a really helpful and practical 'social media assessment' tool, which enables you to test where you are currently positioned within the dimensions of OSML, providing practical understanding of your strengths and weaknesses. For a modest fee, you also have the opportunity to get a more differentiated picture that allows comparisons with the global template, so you can benchmark yourself and your organization.

The Center for the Future of Organization provides an online portal where you can find more information and take the assessment. The link is futureorg.org/osmlsurvey.

Bringing this back to you, the leader

A key takeaway for me when undertaking research for *Get Social* has been on discussing and exploring the difference between 'digital' and 'social'.

The digital technologies, including social media technologies, are purely enablers. They enable and facilitate 'social' behaviours, which include collaboration, co-creation, one-to-many conversations and the sharing of knowledge. Embedding the technologies is the first step; the biggest challenge is creating a culture that permits and encourages 'social literacy'.

From a leadership perspective, facilitating social literacy behaviours has a number of implications. For some it means the letting go of traditional thinking and tactics – 'pushed down', command and control, knowledge held by only a few – and instead embracing tactics and thinking around 'pulling together', made by many, co-created, sharing, transparency and open minds to new ways of operating.

Such change does not happen overnight, and nor should it. But the intention to optimize and leverage the benefits of the wisdom of the crowd and collaboration to create a more 'socially literate' culture should be firmly on the agenda.

Determining social media literacy

I have mentioned being 'socially literate', but what exactly does it encompass? From my perspective, it is the social behaviours facilitated by the technology:

- collaboration;
- customer or employee engagement (both internal and external customers);
- co-creation;
- communication;
- engagement;
- sharing;
- transparency;
- accessibility.

In a McKinsey & Co paper by Roland Deiser and Sylvain Newton, 'Six Social Media Skills Every Leader Needs', they include a model, 'The six dimensions of social media-literate leaders', which considers six 'roles' and related responsibilities (Deiser and Newton, 2013).

Personal level

Producer	Distributor	Recipient
Leaders need to know how to create compelling rich multimedia content people will respond to. They must excel in co-creation and collaboration – the new currency of the social media world.	Leaders need a deep understanding of the nature of the various social media tools, and the dynamics they unleash, as participatory dissemination can be viral and is naturally hard to control. Mastering the combination of the logic of broadcast and participatory media will be critical.	Social media creates unprecedented information overflow and the demise of editorial filters. Leaders need to become sophisticated in managing and leveraging the multiple channels of incoming communication as well as the ability to assess the relevance and factuality of information.

Strategic/organizational level

Adviser	Architect	Analyst
With social media activity proliferating at every level inside and outside the organization, leaders need to become tutors and strategic orchestrators of all such activities within the realm of their control.	Leaders need to make sure that their organizations are designed to encourage self-organized horizontal discourse and exchange. At the same time they must mitigate the risks of irresponsible use through smart policies and vertical accountability frameworks.	The revolution in communication and connectivity technology is not over; it is rather accelerating. Leaders need to understand the nature of this revolution, recognize emerging trends, and leverage the resulting opportunities.

This model includes a number of aspects that we have covered in this and earlier chapters, and may be useful for you to consider, particularly from a 'how do we do this' and 'gap analysis' perspective. Again, you will find access to deeper explanations via www.futureorg.org/sixskills.

Strategic focus for you and your leadership team

The bulk of this book focuses on you the leader getting to grips with social, and providing practical tools, structure and frameworks for you to get social. As stated at the outset of this chapter, I am referencing the organizational implications, not with the intention of providing a solution, but rather, and as highlighted in the six dimensions model, as they are inextricably linked to you, as a leader within the organization.

It is highly likely that digital transformation in some format – digital, mobile and social – is already part of your strategic conversations. If it is not, or perhaps the focus is purely on the implementation of the 'social technology' rather than the 'social literacy' such technologies enable, then there is work to be done. I urge you to immerse yourself more fully in understanding the organizational implications of social literacy. Or at least, with your leadership team, work through the questions already raised at the outset of this chapter and those towards the end of this chapter.

In the CapGemini 'How Digital Leaders Outperform Their Peers in Every Industry' report, it cites examples of engaging the organization and external audiences at scale. It showcases leaders using an array of digital channels such as web, video and social networks to generate continuous two-way communications, such as Richard Branson for example, CEO of Virgin Group, encouraging customers to get in touch using a custom hashtag via Twitter (CapGemini Consulting, 2017). A quick review of T-Mobile CEO John Legere's activity will provide you with highly engaging content, rich media and one-to-one, one-to-many conversations, which will also illustrate how this can be done.

Of course, you are not operating in isolation and, as part of a leadership team, or the CEO with ultimate responsibility for leading the leaders, there are people for you to 'pull together' and collaborate with to make things happen. You may want to champion social literacy or make it a strategic focus across the business, or it may be that you have a chief digital officer on board, who is already tasked with that mission.

Optimize 'social literacy' by collaborating and co-creating with your leadership team. Create a 'think tank', a social media literacy task force, and allocate specific roles and responsibilities. Use Roland Deiser's survey or assessment tool, and assess your strengths and weaknesses around social media technology and social literacy against the six dimensions; understand the gaps and plan to take action to remedy any shortfalls.

Some in the team may be more 'socially literate' than others, so learn from them, understand what you have from a competency perspective and create a platform to share knowledge and transfer skills.

In Chapter 5, I mentioned Stephen Kelly, CEO of Sage Group plc, and his social activity on Twitter and LinkedIn – it is interesting to see that Steve Hare, Chief Financial Officer (CFO) of Sage Group plc, is also highly active on Twitter, as is Blair Crump, President of Sage

Group plc. Whilst each has their own voice, there has clearly been a concerted decision to engage some of the leadership team on social media, along with the brand and customer support activity. Their content across their social channels focuses on thought leadership pieces on LinkedIn around the start-up, small to medium enterprise (SME) space, and entrepreneurship, as well as bringing in the social element of conversing and congratulating Sage employees and customers and commenting on or sharing general insights relating to activities, developments and events happening within Sage. They also facilitate discussions around social causes they care about, such as their foundation and charity runs.

How is social currently working in your C-suite?

Social literacy across leadership teams and organizations is going to differ from business to business. However, what is important as a leader is for you to question what the strategic social digital vision is; where the plan is to help you execute it; who is involved and how you are going to upskill those involved to be as effective as possible. Your strategic social digital plan needs champions and deliverable tactics and, importantly, accountability to make it happen:

- Is there a clear strategic social media vision within and across the business?
- Is there a clear social media roadmap within and across the business? Tactically, how will you achieve it? If there is, who is championing it?
- Are key leaders involved?
- What does social literacy look like across your C-suite?
- How competent is your leadership team in social literacy?
- What are you going to do to upskill those involved to be as effective as possible?
- If training is required, what does that look like? Is it, as is the case with PwC and Lego, that social media training is mandatory

for team members, and that there are exams and certification and internal benchmarks?

- Is the CEO blogging?
- Are other leaders/thought leaders/experts and beyond sharing their knowledge, both internally and externally?
- Are there specific topics that are closely linked to specific executives, enabling each to focus on thought leadership in a specific area? For example: marketing, strategy, technology and innovation, customer service or brand. If you are making incredible achievements in any of these areas, then who is tasked with sharing those insights to grow authority and trust?
- Or is it rather an audience focus, as is the case with the Sage Group plc example, where they are collectively focusing on the start-up, SME and entrepreneur messaging?
- How are you supporting each other with accountability?

To wrap up

As we have explored in this chapter, social media activity is not something an organization does just for the sake of doing social media (or because everyone else is!) but rather to deliver on business objectives, ideally as part of a well-defined strategy to assist in driving real competitive advantage.

The better the culture, and the more 'socially literate' a business is, then the more likely it is that social media will succeed, as good communications start from within.

Where better for those good communications, collaboration and co-creation to exist than within the leadership team, with a role model 'leader' acting as a beacon of 'social literacy', to inspire and motivate best practice across the organization? As a leader, whether you are the leader of the leaders, or part of the team, where better to start than with yourself to educate and inspire others?

The previous chapters of *Get Social* have hopefully provided you with ideas, reference points and logical reasons to 'get social'. The next chapter, your 90-day social media plan is where you take action.

Grab some pens and lots of paper, get your laptop, your phone and get online… you are about to take action and 'get social'.

Remember these three things

1 Social media technologies do not in and of themselves create the environment for social literacy. Culture, training and strategic direction are fundamental for the development of social literacy.
2 Social media is a key component of digital transformation.
3 Social media has the potential to plug in to each of the different business units to assist with delivering against objectives.

Take action

- Review or develop your strategic social digital vision, understand where you are now and create a clear social media roadmap to enable social literacy to develop and thrive across your organization.
- Remember, you are not alone; collaborate and co-create with your team and employees. Create a social media 'think tank'.
- Start. Everything begins with small steps. But it doesn't start until it starts.

References

CapGemini Consulting in association with MITSloan Management (2017) [accessed 30 November 2017] The Digital Advantage: How Digital Leaders Outperform Their Peers in Every Industry [Online] https://www.capgemini.com/wp-content/uploads/2017/07/The_Digital_Advantage__How_Digital_Leaders_Outperform_their_Peers_in_Every_Industry.pdf

Deiser, Roland and Newton, Sylvain (2013) [accessed 30 November 2017] Six Social-Media Skills Every Leader Needs, *McKinsey Quarterly*, February 2013 [Online] https://www.mckinsey.com/industries/high-tech/our-insights/six-social-media-skills-every-leader-needs

Goffee, R and Jones, G (2015) *Why Should Anyone Work Here? What it takes to create an authentic organization*, Harvard Business Review Press, United States

Harrysson, M, Schoder, D and Tavakoli, A (2016) [accessed 30 November 2017] The Evolution of Social Technologies, *McKinsey Quarterly*, June 2016 [Online] https://www.mckinsey.com/industries/high-tech/our-insights/the-evolution-of-social-technologies

Holmes Noble (2017) [accessed 30 November 2017] The DNA of a Modern CEO [Online] https://www.holmesnoble.com/wp-content/uploads/2017/08/Holmes-Noble-The-DNA-of-a-modern-CEO.pdf

Miller, Rachel (2013) [accessed 30 November 2017] Who's Using What for Internal Social Media? 400 ESN Case Studies [Online] http://www.allthingsic.com/list

07
90-day plan

Creating your 90-day personal social media strategy and plan

You, like me, may read a lot of non-fiction, business books. Across most of the ones I read, I scribble notes, insert Post-its and earmark aspects to come back to, often with the intention of workshopping some of the learnings. In fact, many books include suggested action points and exercises within chapters. However, it's very rare that I stop mid-chapter to get out the pens and paper and take action.

Of course, once the book is finished and it's packed with Post-its and scribbled handwritten notes, whilst my every intention is to work through it again and revisit each chapter and undertake the suggested actions, realistically, I'm back to my day job and the next shiny new book is enticing me with its potential. Rather than diving deeper and taking action, I satisfy myself that I've read the book. I walk away with the surface-level gems and continue on my merry way.

It is exactly for this reason that this chapter is purposely structured differently to the others in this book. Effectively, this chapter is 100 per cent dedicated to revisiting all the previous suggested actions and pulling them into one place. Creating a practical, comprehensive, DIY coaching-style implementation programme that, over a 90-day period, walks you through suggested steps and exercises to assist you in getting fit for purpose and, importantly, walking the walk, taking action and getting started.

Realistically, there is a lot to achieve in 90 days, and realistically, a number of the tasks may stretch beyond the time frames I've set. However, the main focus is on having a 90-day plan, getting started and taking action.

A number of years ago, during my time as a consultant to professional services firms, assisting them with business development and growth strategies, one of the key 'diseases' we would talk about with clients was the terrible FTI, otherwise known as 'failure to implement'. Since learning about the FTI disease all those years ago, I still see it everywhere. Training courses, away days, planning sessions. I've even fallen prey to it myself a number of times. After all, it doesn't matter how fired up one is to make a change, start a project or take action; unless you actually do something, then FTI has set in.

On a positive note, the more you do implement, the more results you are likely to see, the more momentum that builds and, therefore, the more likely you are to keep at it. A key way to combat FTI is via accountability. If you are highly disciplined, then it may be enough to be accountable to yourself, or perhaps you will involve some external support, perhaps a colleague, your assistant, coach or even a family member.

Whilst I have endeavoured to pull everything into one place for you, and create a comprehensive programme, it is down to you to do the work, put in the effort, do the thinking and find the resource required to get your plan down and then bring it to life.

As well as the programme, I'll be continuously updating useful resources and other relevant materials via the www.getsocial.site online resource. You will find templates of the frameworks set out in the following programme there too, together with spreadsheets and other resources that don't fit into the scope of a hard copy book.

On www.getsocial.site, you will also find a private network for readers of this book and for leaders or aspiring leaders who want to ask questions, share ideas, stories and wins, or just generally tune in to learn what others are doing in the social media space. I invite you to jump in and join the conversation.

In Chapter 8, and at the end of the book in the Appendix, you will find reference to a number of real-world interviews with social CEOs and leaders. I'll continue to interview leaders around the 'social leadership' topic over the coming months and the www.getsocial.site will become the hub for more interviews. If you would like to share your story with me, be sure to contact me directly or visit the site and let me know how you're doing.

In the meantime, let's take a look at how I've structured the programme.

What your 90-day programme covers

Weeks 1–3: Getting fit for purpose

- Where are you now? Where do you want to be?

- What is the purpose? Determining your why.

- Understanding your role in the context of organizational activity and what resources are available to you.

Weeks 4–9: Getting social

- Developing your personal brand.

- Selecting and developing your personal platforms.

- Developing your content strategy and tactics.

Weeks 10–12: Getting results

- Measuring what matters.

- Accountability and progress check in

The above framework is designed with the consideration that you're a busy executive who is going to have to build in the time to work on this programme to 'get social'. Given that I have no idea where you are in your endeavours of 'being social', I'm making the assumption that by reading this book, you're looking for a resource that will provide you with a practical roadmap.

I've kept timings fairly tight, to keep momentum going, motivating you to stick to the task. Whilst I've structured the programme into three chunks, it is by no means linear. You will note that it follows a natural progression in line with my Smart Social Focus Model (Plan, Listen, Analyse, Engage and Measure – PLAEM) that we covered in Chapter 5. You will also note that a number of the exercises throughout the book have been pulled into this one place – centralizing everything and making them part of the programme.

Accountability and progress check-ins

I have built in accountability and progress checks to keep you motivated and inspired. These allow you to measure your progress. As your understanding, application and activity develop, the progress check enables you to track them.

You have probably attended several leadership development courses stressing the importance of stopping to notice the small wins. An analogy I use to explain why accountability and progress checks matter is that of climbing Mount Kilimanjaro. The objective is simple, to reach the summit. However, standing at the bottom and looking forward, it may seem like a huge task, even a bit overwhelming. Yet to get to the summit you're not going to go all out and conquer it all in one sprint, but rather, you are going to map out the kilometres and, based on a number of factors such as stops to replenish resources, sleep, food and management of mountain sickness etc, you are going to chunk the task of climbing that mountain into realistically doable sections. When you hit each base camp, the reflection that you have progressed and made it so far is what motivates the next leg of the climb.

Whilst you may not consider 'getting social' as adventurous as climbing a mountain, glancing through the programme you may be feeling like there is a lot to it, and be asking yourself how you have time even to start thinking about it. It may seem like a huge task, one that is even a bit overwhelming.

We know that, psychologically, the brain likes to win. Even if progress is small, it is still moving forward. Also note that the 'tasks' I've included relate to those discussed throughout the book. However, it may indeed be that you want to include wider organizational aspects such as alignment with organizational social media activity, creating a C-suite or social media leadership think tank, or implementing social media training across the entire organization. So you can edit accordingly.

To make life simple for you, the templates for all tables and checklists in this programme will be stored in the resources area on the www.getsocial.site. Or, of course, you can tailor and create your own.

Let's start

What's the purpose? Determining your why

You have picked up this book for a reason. Perhaps it was gifted to you, perhaps you have been a curious cat about how to get going with social media for a while, perhaps you have heard some good news stories from peers or colleagues and you're keen to give it a go. Or, perhaps, there is another driver. For example, remember, the reference I shared earlier, CEO Roberto Sallouti taking to social media to assist with transparency to aid reputation management:

> We had this reputation of being a secretive, closed institution and we wanted to change that, to be seen as transparent, communicative. And the way to do that was through social media.

Whatever your driver, I want you to take some time to get really clear about 'why' you want to 'get social'.

As a leader, if it is about connecting with customers or employees to engage and build trust, then of course these channels provide you with a simple and transparent way to share your message.

However, in just the same way as we discussed in Chapters 5 and 6, simply being on social media is not in itself going to engender trust – but engaging, answering questions, asking questions and being open and transparent and human, is. Remember, the channels are purely channels; what you pour into them is what matters.

As a leader, you may already have absolute clarity on your 'purpose'. Why you do what you do, why you lead the way you do, why you work for the organization you do. If you are not clear on your purpose, I urge you to take some time to get clear about the following:

- What are your values, beliefs and passions?
- Why would someone want to follow you?
- How do you inspire others?
- What cause or purpose do you champion?
- What is your purpose for being social?

Determining your purpose is going to help steer your messaging, your content creation, who you tune in to and connect with – and it is highly likely to align with your organization. For example, remember, Jack Parsons, CEO of Big Youth Group? His clear focus is 'to improve the odds for young people'. His message is consistent with his mission.

Beyond 'being social', when it comes to finding your 'why', personally, I love the work of bestselling author Simon Sinek, author of *Start with Why* and *Leaders Eat Last*. If you're looking for some inspiration it is worth spending 30 minutes tuning into his 'Finding Your Why' talk on YouTube (Sinek, 2009). In this short video, and throughout his books, he illustrates the successes of organizations and people who focus on their 'why' – sharing beliefs and purpose, rather than merely focusing on the 'what' they do and 'how' they do it. Effectively, sharing what you believe in, being authentic and building trust, a key theme we have touched on continuously throughout this book.

Remember, at this stage we're fact finding and so it is useful to take those same questions that I ask you to ask yourself above, and ask the same questions about you to some peers, family or friends – people you trust and whose opinion you value. Position them as follows:

- What would you say are my values, beliefs and passions?
- Why would someone want to follow me?
- How do I inspire others?
- What cause or purpose do I champion?
- What would be my purpose for being social?

I did this exercise myself; I emailed the questions to a handful of people and asked for their viewpoint. It is very interesting what comes up. I urge you to do it.

The outcomes from this exercise will assist you with developing your personal brand, what you want to be known for and how you translate that across various media. (See the 'Getting Social' section of this programme.)

Weeks 1–3: Getting fit for purpose

Where you are now… where do you want to be?

Day 1, week 1, let's set a baseline. Simply score yourself out of 10 relating to where you feel you currently sit. If it is zero, then that's okay, as we're starting out. This forms the baseline for progress over the next 90 days.

Accountability and progress check 1 – setting your baseline

How are you doing?	Score out of 10
Social media and content plan in place	
Overall social media competency	
Active on social media daily	
Engaging with customers/employees via social media	
Activity 'tuning in' and listening daily on social media	
Metrics and ROI tracking in place to measure social media activity	
Enjoying 'being social' on social media	
Social media role model/influencer across the organization	
Baseline total score:	

How do you show up?

First things first, a little bit of desk research to figure out how you currently show up. Spend a few minutes 'googling' yourself, your name, your name and title, your name and organization:

- What do people find when they currently search for you?
- How recent are any articles? Are they from years ago – or right up to the current moment?
- Are there any elements that you feel are missing?
- Are you happy with what's out there?

Review the findings and assess where social media is impacting your online visibility. At the same time, google a few of your peers or colleagues or mentors who do social really well. How do they compare? Ask peers you respect what they think of social media and whether they are active and why.

Whilst googling, spend some time searching terms around 'Social CEO' or social and C-suite, Top 100 CEOs on Social, and explore generally what others are doing. Take a look at various references I have supplied for you throughout this book, and get a general and broader feel for what is going on with social media and leadership.

Review your online visibility

In line with finding out how you currently 'show up', consider other outposts where you are visible. Such platforms may include your organization's website, intranet, blog or any other communication channel where you have a profile.

Review what it says about you and also don't forget to review any photos or profile pictures too. Again, review whether everything is current and correct. Are you happy with what's out there? Is it a true reflection of you?

Consider your digital footprint. Assess where you are right now with your digital footprint, what it looks like, how you currently 'show up' and then take action to influence it so that what's out there is current and positions you as chief storyteller or key thought leader.

Next, let's take a look at your LinkedIn profile

Whilst you may not be active on LinkedIn, out of all the social networks it is the one where it is highly likely you have already created a profile.

When we discussed LinkedIn in Chapter 3, I explained that you have your LinkedIn profile that is visible to those logged into LinkedIn, and you also have a public profile that is visible to those who are not logged into LinkedIn.

My advice when searching how you show up on LinkedIn is to go 'incognito' via private browsing. This is an option you can enable via the menu in the top-right corner of your web browser. This way, your browser should not detect any previous LinkedIn logins and you will get to see exactly what appears if someone was simply searching for you, without being connected. In fact, this public profile is likely to come up in Google searches too.

Again, assess the following:

- What do people find when they currently search for you?
- How recent are any articles or posts you have shared? Are they from years ago – or right up to the current moment?
- Are there any elements that you feel are missing?
- How is your profile pic?
- Are you happy with what is out there?

Assessing the findings

The objective of the 'How do I show up' review is really for you to determine how happy you are with the current state of play.

It may be that you are totally happy – and if so, great. Alternatively, it may throw up some questions and identify some gaps. For example, if you are the CEO or senior leader in the C-suite and there isn't anywhere on your website for customers to find out a little more about those managing the business, does that need to be remedied?

Similarly, on internal-facing systems, is there a platform for you the CEO or leader to share and communicate to your employees who you are and what you stand for?

Understanding how social media is working within the organization

The next part of the programme is for you to get an understanding as to how social media currently plays out within your organization. Asking the usual what, who, how, when and why questions:

- What is the strategy?
- How is it structured?

- How does it work operationally?
- Who is responsible for the activity?
- Who is involved?
- How is it performing?
- What are we learning?

The intention is for you to get a grasp of what's happening. You don't need to become an expert in social media strategy across the organization, but as a leader, steering or as part of the leadership team, it's about joining up the dots and ensuring that there is sufficient understanding.

In Chapter 2, we discussed the following tasks:

- Become fully conversant with your customer demographics and include them as part of management information so that you can analyse trends. It may be that your organization is already tracking such data. What is important for you to uncover is what insights such data uncovers. Are you seeing more customers engaging with your organization via social media? If so, which channels? I recall recently tweeting a talk by McKinsey, delivered by Facebook Live. One can assume that their data is showing that their audience is active on that channel and therefore that medium is an effective one to engage via. What insights is your data advising you of and how is that shaping the way you and your organization communicate?

- Determine which social channels your audiences are using so you are clear on which channels to tune in to.

- Leverage the learning from data and insights gleaned from your organization's social media activity. For example, if your focus is to engage with customers, and the insights show that all your customers are on Instagram, then such insight would determine exactly which channel it would be important for you to participate on.

This exercise from Chapter 1 may prove useful in understanding where both you and your organization sit with regards to social media from a strategic and tactical perspective.

Does your business have:

A defined business strategy with KPIs (key performance indicators)?	YES/NO
Focused goals for social media/digital marketing?	YES/NO
A blog/news channel on your website?	YES/NO
A 'growth' mindset – open to new ideas and new trends?	YES/NO
A basic understanding of the benefits of social media and digital communications?	YES/NO
A content plan in place – where to source ideas for relevant and compelling content?	YES/NO
Plans to actively listen to what customers say about your business?	YES/NO
A customer engagement programme in place?	YES/NO

Now over to you. Do you have:

A basic understanding of the benefits of social media and digital communications?	YES/NO
A social media engagement strategy with KPIs?	YES/NO
Focused goals for your social media activity?	YES/NO
A blog/news channel where you share your expertise/views?	YES/NO
A growth mindset – open to new ideas and new trends?	YES/NO
A content plan in place to create relevant and compelling content?	YES/NO
The means to tune in in 'real time' and listen to what your customers say about your business?	YES/NO

As illustrated above, the first chunk of your 90-day plan is really a deeper dive into how things currently stand, for you and your organization. It is about becoming informed and aware of where you are right now, how things are working and any insights that may steer your personal activity going forward.

Week 4 assessment: getting fit for purpose checklist

Action	Done
What is the purpose? Determining your why – questions answered	
What is the purpose? Determining your why – questions answered by six selected others	
How you show up – questions/gap analysis task	

(continued)

Action	Done
How you show up – Google activity task	
Research social CEOs and read references supplied – understand the landscape	
Talk to peers, colleagues, mentors about their views on social media	
How you show up – assess online visibility generally	
How you show up – undertake a LinkedIn review	
Assess the findings from the suggested fact-finding tasks and develop actions points	
Understand how social works within and across the organization	

Weeks 4–9: Getting social

Developing your personal brand

At the outset, I asked you to work on your 'why', your purpose. These aspects form the central part of your personal brand. Sure, you are the CEO or leader, but what about you? Who are you, what do you stand for, what is your mission and what needs to come across when people see your profiles on social media? We are talking about your profile picture, cover photos and the words that make up your profiles.

When determining the outposts for your personal brand, it may be that you are stretching beyond social media channels. You can see from Figure 7.1 that there are a number of channels for you to consider where your personal brand sits.

In just the same way that a 'brand' has values and beliefs, so too do you. As a leader within the organization, you are highly likely to be aligned with the beliefs of your brand and organization, and therefore, it may be simply a case of you extending those values and beliefs into your own personal brand activity. After all, you are a walking, talking brand ambassador.

Key questions around your personal brand:

- What is your purpose?
- What do you want to be known for? If for thought leadership, in what area?

Figure 7.1 An integrated approach to your online platforms

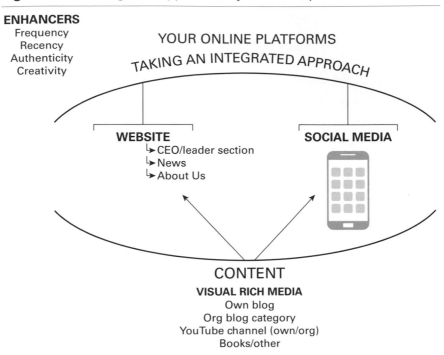

- Who do you want to inspire? Employees, customers?

- What image do you want to portray?

- What are your messages?

- Where can people find out more about you? (Personal website, organization's website, page on the website, YouTube channel etc.)

- Will any tangible assets be required to assist with building your personal brand?

- Sense check with others. If relevant, speak to your communications, social media team or agency to understand the organizational social media objectives and how your personal activity could align. Research and gain insights into what other leaders and CEOs are doing.

Another quick exercise you may find useful in helping you to define your purpose:

- three adjectives that describe your values;

- three words that define your personality;

- three things you are the 'go-to person' on;
- three audiences you want to capture the attention of.

Selecting and developing your personal platforms

From the insights gleaned in your fact-finding phase, it may be very evident as to which channels your customers participate on. For example, let's say, as is the case with John Legere, CEO of T-Mobile, your audience is on a number of channels: Facebook, Twitter, Instagram and Snapchat. The channels you select should be the ones your audiences participate on. Ideally, aligned with your objectives. Go back to that 'why' question – around what it is that you want to achieve and determining the 'what' and the 'how'.

'What'

- brand (awareness, reputation);
- business intelligence (listening, tuning in);
- customer loyalty (building relationships, loyalty, advocacy);
- employee engagement (building relationships, loyalty, advocacy);
- supporting business-wide initiatives (eg launch of a new product).

As part of your personal strategy, we also need to consider the following important tactical aspects.

'How'

- Which channels you are going to show up on?
- What is the purpose of each channel?
- Who are you going to follow on each channel?
- What are you going to create for each channel (content)?
- How are you going to engage?
- How often will you be visible (frequency and schedule)?
- Who (you alone or are you working with a team)?

- What if… (reputation management, escalation, crisis management, guidelines, processes)?
- What are you going to measure?

Chapter 3 outlines the most common social media channels and provides you with practical tips for optimizing the set-up and activity. Your task is to:

- Review any customer data, analysis and insights.
- Determine where your audience is.
- Do some research into which channels and platforms are relevant for you.
- Select the relevant channels and set-up and optimize.

Given you are a leader and business professional, then LinkedIn is really a necessity and the Pulse publishing platform enables you to share thought leadership pieces and build professional connections. You can also share your message to employees (provided your employees are following you), and prospective employees and customers, partners and other stakeholders. I urge you to audit your LinkedIn profile to ensure that it is fully optimized and engaging.

Remember, your LinkedIn profile should be more in line with a personal website than a CV. It enables you to include rich media, images, slides. Ensure that you are continuing your personal brand messaging across this channel too.

Once you have chosen your channels, then it's a case of growing your audience.

Growing an audience on social media is a bit of a long game. Once your contacts know that you are on social, then connections will organically start to build. It's highly likely you already have a significant amount of connections via LinkedIn. You can include, let's say, your Twitter profile and any other social media profiles into your LinkedIn profile to advise your connections that you are now on Twitter. Also, there are ways that you can bring your contacts into Twitter and automatically connect with them. The social networks have been designed to be social, so when you are setting them up, they give you options to connect with your connections.

Once you've got a base, you can then simply start following those you are interested in tuning in to, getting involved with hashtags and conversations, sharing, commenting and generally engaging. All this generally builds your following in an authentic way.

Other ways to engage

- Ask open questions and seek opinion – drive engagement and openness.
- I can't express enough the importance of listening. Listen, learn – gain insight from your audience.
- Learn about future challenges as it can help you shape your future business strategy and tactics.
- Don't be afraid to show the good and the challenging.
- Give value – always be helping not always be 'closing'.
- Be where your audience is. Spend time where you want to build and engage a community and put your efforts there.
- Be a leader. Look ahead and produce thought-provoking content around the challenges your sector faces now and potentially in the future – seek out the opinions of others.
- Remember, they are two-way connections. Look for opportunities that create conversations.

Whilst we are still impressed when we see an account with thousands of followers, my advice is that whilst having a broader base can be useful for amplifying key messages, from a leadership perspective focus first on the quality of the connection. Being active on the channel organically builds followers. As outlined above, focus on quality of connection over quantity.

Listening and tuning in

Another key aspect of 'getting social' is tuning in and listening to what's happening on the channels.

Once you've set up channels, then initially start by simply listening in. Search #hashtags, people, brands, competitors, colleagues, influencers. Spend time watching and learning. Have someone from your social media team, or a colleague involved with social media, on hand so that you've got a reliable 'go to' person to ask questions to. There are no stupid questions. Your objective is to get really comfortable with the platforms:

- Select 10 relevant accounts and follow them for a few days.
- Spend 15 minutes each day tuning in to get a feel for the platforms.

Depending on where you are at with 'Getting Social', you may want or need to dedicate some time into your programme for some basic one-to-one training. The platforms are fairly intuitive, but a safe pair of hands to guide you through set-up and assist with any questions and show you the ropes is always really useful in the early days.

Developing your content strategy and tactics

As stated earlier, determining your 'why', your purpose, your mission, helps to steer your content. However, for you as leader or CEO, from a content perspective it is likely that such steer will encompass a focus on brand, reputation, thought leadership and customer and employee engagement.

We covered content planning extensively in Chapter 4, so in this programme we will recap on the practicalities:

Map out what happens in your world

Month	Your Activity	Organization Activity	General/ Seasonal
January	Speaking engagement – Japan		
February	Radio interview	New product launch	Valentine's Day
March	Budget review		International Women's Day
April	Quarterly analysis review/report		
May		Big promotional campaign begins	

(continued)

Month	Your Activity	Organization Activity	General/ Seasonal
June	ABC Expo Madrid – keynote		
July	Quarterly analysis review/report		
August	Judging ABC awards selecting shortlist		
September	Suppliers forum	Big promotional campaign ends	
October	ABC Awards Event – sponsoring	New office opening in Spain	
November	Internal forecast report	Recruitment drive	
December			Holiday season

Mapping out what happens in your world assists with determining what content you have to work with on a daily, weekly, monthly, even quarterly basis – assisting you with balancing the mix of curated, repurposed, created and spontaneous.

Whilst you don't want your activity to be robotic or formulaic, instead see the content planning as ensuring you are not missing any key areas that offer opportunity to align with both your purpose and the wider organizational purpose. (Indeed, they may be exactly the same.)

40% Curated	30% Repurposed	20% Created	10% Spontaneous
Curating and sharing others' content that you find interesting or relevant. (Of course, you can always add your own personal twist to this – for example, by adding a comment when retweeting something.)	Repurposing and recycling content you already have. <ul><li>Blog posts – turning written posts into live streams or vice versa</li><li>Keynotes</li><li>Articles</li><li>Interviews</li></ul>	Your unique content. Thought leadership pieces. <ul><li>New blog posts</li><li>New articles</li><li>Live streams</li><li>Video</li><li>Interviews</li><li>Product launches</li><li>Campaigns</li><li>Keynotes</li></ul>	Leaving space in your content pipeline for spontaneous slice-of-life content. Sharing real-world relevant stuff as it happens.

Of course, you may want to consider a mixture of the type of content you facilitate. Again, this may track back to your specific purpose. If your objective is to educate and inspire – then the types of content you will be focused on will differ from those in the promote and entertain sections, which may be more aligned with organizational activity:

Entertain	Educate	Inspire	Promote
• Competitions	• Guides	• Interviews with	• Case studies
• Games	• E-books	influencers	• Product
• Fun viral videos	• Thought	• Reviews	features and
• Quizzes	leadership	• Testimonials	benefits
• Keynote	articles	• Keynote	• Promotional
video/slides	• Reports	video/slides	offers
	• Press releases	• Content that	
	• How to/demos	inspires you that	
	• Keynote	you feel compelled	
	video/slides	to share	

These lists are not prescriptive, but rather, I have included them to assist with opening your thinking to the different types of content and the purpose behind your content plan – asking yourself the following questions:

- What is my message?
- What is my authentic voice?
- What am I looking to achieve?
- What content is going to fit with my purpose?
- What is important to my audience?
- What content is going to be useful to my audience?
- What questions have they raised?
- What do they want to know about?
- What do I want them to know about?
- What do we get asked all the time?

Week 9 assessment: Getting fit for purpose checklist

Action	Done
Determined how my purpose fits.	
Reviewed analysis relating to where our audiences are on social.	
Selected the relevant channels and set up/optimized.	
Tuned in to 10 accounts. Ran searches and dedicated at last 15 minutes a day for a week for listening.	
Attacked my content plan.	
Reviewed three 'what's happening in my world' and 'what's topical' and mapped it out.	
Reviewed the different types of content and decided on tactics.	
Reviewed content that is already in place and have determined how it can be updated or repurposed to extend or resurrect its life (considered video as highly engaging).	
Set up meetings with relevant teams to gain insights and support.	
Explored what's going on in the business from a content/thought leadership perspective.	
Blocked out time in my diary for content creation or capture. Started with 15 minutes twice a week to capture ideas and an hour for creation. It won't just magically happen unless I set aside time to make it happen.	
Reviewed the social media guidelines within the organization. Now familiar with what is suggested regarding content, tone of voice and brand messaging.	

Weeks 10–12: Getting results

- Measuring what matters.
- Accountability and progress check in.

When it comes to ROI and measuring what matters, I would certainly encourage you to gain an understanding from your organization as to how they go about measuring their social media activity, and understanding how your activity can be measured.

Aspects you can map into measuring your activity as CEO or leader:

- Increase brand awareness:
  - Are you growing *relevant* followers?
- Establish credibility and trust:
  - Are you getting endorsements/shares from *influential* people?
  - How is your audience responding to these influencers?
  - Are those influencers extending the reach of your audience?
- Connect with your audience:
  - Is your audience responding well to your content?
  - Is the content you share encouraging *engagement*?
  - What levels of shares, reach and discussion is your content achieving?
- Find new leads/drive sales:
  - Is social activity bringing people back to your website/landing page?
  - Have you achieved a certain amount of sign-ups/downloads?
  - How is social helping you to retain/engage customers/employees?

Not all of these aspects may be relevant. But they provide you with at least a starting point for practical discussion to enable you to determine what you need to consider.

Accountability and progress check 2 – week 12

How are you doing?	Score out of 10
Social media and content plan in place	
Overall social media competency	
Active on social media daily	
Engaging with customers/employees via social media	
Activity 'tuning in' and listening daily on social media	
Metrics and ROI tracking in place to measure social media activity	
Enjoying 'being social' on social media	
Social media role model/influencer across the organization	
Baseline total score:	

As stated at the outset, this programme is here to initiate the start of your social media activity. It purposely focuses on you the leader, and your activity. In Chapter 6 the entire chapter focuses on social media strategy and activity from an organizational perspective. I have purposely steered away from including that aspect in this 90-day programme.

See it as a starting point – getting your 'get social' conversation started and steering you in the right direction. Adapt it as required and make it yours. The key objective is that you take action along the way, and get started to ensure you don't catch a nasty dose of FTI.

Reference

Simon Sinek (2009) [accessed 30 November 2017] Start With Why, *YouTube* [Online] https://www.youtube.com/watch?v=tNvfOfGTO6c

08
Learning from others

When writing this book I thought it would not only be useful to share the lessons I had learnt from the years of training, coaching and consulting, but also to hear views, opinion, experience and insights around social media, from real-world leaders. Throughout *Get Social* I have shared some snippets from the interviews that steer this chapter. The interviews with CEOs, founders or senior leaders can be found in the Appendix. Without exception, each of the leaders you will read about in the Appendix were contacted via social media, either Twitter or LinkedIn.

At the time of writing, there are a few CEOs and leaders who, whilst they have agreed to share their opinion and experiences and are committed to doing so, have missed the publishing deadline. However, once those interviews are finalized, even though they will not make the content of this book, their opinions and insights will be shared via the book's dedicated website www.getsocial.site. In fact, my intention is to continue to seek opinion, experiences and insight from other leaders and CEOs as to how they are embracing and leveraging social media. I hope I will therefore be growing an insightful and useful repository of knowledge to share.

It is also useful to reference another resource you may find both interesting and useful. Over the past four years, Damian Corbet, founder of The Social C-Suite, has interviewed a number of CEOs. On The Social C-Suite site, you will find at least another 20 or so interviews, from leaders across a variety of sectors. Each interview uncovers how they are using social and how social media is helping them to be a more effective leader. As well as hearing from the CEOs and leaders I interviewed, I'm sure you will find Damian's interviews to be another useful resource to explore. Simply visit www.thesocialcsuite.net.

For now, let me first introduce you to the CEOs, leaders and founders I interviewed. The book is titled *Get Social* and so I wanted to share insights from those leaders I was aware of who were definitely living proof of using social media effectively. As you will see, those interviewed all 'get social' in slightly different ways. Whilst there are a number of similarities with how these leaders view social media, from the point of valuing its importance as a communication resource there are differences in how they are using the channels. Some are using platforms in ways that others are not – or perhaps, are not yet!

I'm pleased with the variety of tone, enthusiasm, confidence and adoption. For me, it evidences social media in a transparent way. I have retained views that may sometimes seem a little negative. But from my perspective, that makes the interviews all the more authentic. Social media isn't a new shiny thing that we have all fallen in love with. Whilst it manifests opportunities, it also brings challenges that require rethinking the way we operate – and not all of it is positive. The key is to make it work for you in a way that works for you. For each leader that is likely to be different.

Personally, I found the interviews most illuminating. My hope is that there are some useful nuggets and practical takeaways to be gleaned from the varied pool of knowledge and experiences from those who very kindly gave me some of their valuable time to share their views and knowledge. Ultimately, being 'social'.

This chapter provides not the full versions of the interviews, but rather a summary of findings and key takeaways from the learnings of others, and also unites and draws in concepts we have covered in previous chapters. As a little motivation to dive into those full interviews in the Appendix, I have included my favourite 'quote' from each of the CEOs. A little teaser, or motivator, to encourage you to explore further.

Before I move into the summary of findings, first a brief introduction to the CEOs and leaders featured in the interviews, and how and why I came to interview each of them.

The CEOs and leaders interviewed

- John Legere, CEO, T-Mobile
- Caron Bradshaw, CEO, Charity Finance Group (CFG)
- Kevin Burrowes, Head of Clients and Markets, PwC
- Gordon Beattie, President and Founder, Beattie Communications
- Dr Sam Collins, author and CEO at Aspire
- Kevin Roberts, author and former CEO at Saatchi & Saatchi
- Shaa Wasmund MBE, author and Founder of Shaa.Com
- Brian J Dunn, former CEO, Best Buy
- Steve Tappin, CEO, Xinfu

John Legere, CEO, T-Mobile

In pulling this book together, it would have been a disservice not to have included T-Mobile CEO, John Legere.

If you tune into any of John's social media channels, and I mean any – he is on Twitter (5.3 million+ followers), Facebook (222,000+ fans) and has a huge following on Snapchat and Instagram (40,000+ followers) – you will quickly realize he is a truly social CEO.

T-Mobile as a service crosses both B2B and B2C audiences. When we talk about 'leading from the front', John evidences this in creative and erudite ways via his social media channels. His message on social media channels seems to be very clear. He uses social media in the following ways:

- Brand. His output always evidences brand values. In fact, you will never spot him not donning something 'magenta', the T-Mobile brand colour.

- Business performance. The same candid discussions he has during Bloomberg interviews relating to commercial performance, successes and challenges are shared via his social channels.

- Communicating. Generally talking with the T-Mobile community in a very personable, regular-guy way.

- Customer support. If anyone has any gripes, or indeed suggestions for product improvements, he encourages them to get in touch directly with him, sharing his personal email address.

- Competitor watch. He openly talks about what others are doing in the market, openly showcasing that he is keeping a close eye on what competitors are doing.

- Team thanks and support. He regularly thanks and praises T-Mobile team members when they share news about what they are doing, be it a personal charitable activity or an in-store initiative.

- Confidence. As well as market confidence, showing confidence in his teams. He tirelessly defends the T-Mobile teams' efforts and skills.

On Twitter just last week, it came up on my Twitter feed that John Legere was going 'live' on Twitter. Out for a run through Central Park, he encouraged people to come say 'hi': 'I'm out for a run, beautiful day, if you're a runner, no better way to get out and on to the trails. Perfect weather conditions. Come say hi. Got anything to tell me, or ask me – I'm going to be running for a while, so feel free to ask.'

Hundreds of people tuned in, just to say hi, or typically, tweet 'love you John'. If people are looking to switch provider, he answers questions; where people have a gripe, he will advise and ask them to email him and he will get it sorted. Those who come on the live broadcast just to say how happy they are they switched to T-Mobile, he thanks for their custom. Where people say something defamatory about his team or product, he defends, and the community step in to validate his defence. Talk about crowdsourcing! A perfect example of this was when someone jumped on the broadcast and asked, 'When are you going to get your team in the Philippines to speak better English?'

Without being rude or riled, but with a very genuine, down-to-earth manner, he stated (to paraphrase):

> My team in the Philippines are some of the nicest people you could ever meet and are some of the best customer service operatives around. They, like all the T-Mobile customer service team members, are trained to the highest standard and do a great job day in and day out looking after T-Mobile customers. I'm proud of my team in the Philippines for the great work they do as I am of all my customer support team and if you've got a problem that isn't getting resolved, then email me directly John.legere @...

Of course, this response was met with huge support from the hundreds of people on the broadcast, engendering responses like 'We love your customer service team', 'They're the best', or 'Love customer service at T-Mobile, it's the best ever'. This is all done during a 15-minute broadcast, whilst he is out running through the trails in Central Park.

John Legere, as a '#SocialCEO' from my viewpoint, is probably the most active CEO on social that I've witnessed to date. On a Sunday he runs a regular 'Slow Cooker Sunday' live broadcast via Facebook Live. Donning his T-Mobile chef's hat and clothed, in some way, in the obligatory magenta, he literally preps a dish for the slow cooker. On the Saturday, the day before he presents his cooking broadcast, he does a live broadcast whilst shopping for the ingredients and asks the audience to guess what he's going to make! He's got over 1 million subscribers to this regular live social media broadcast.

Regardless of the successes he has heralded at T-Mobile and the much-reported turnaround of fortunes for that business, I suspect that should John Legere ever decide to move somewhere else, which would at this time seem like he would have to have a total blood transfusion to remove the magenta from his veins, or if he even chose to retire from the business world, he has become such an influential 'social' personality that his 'social legend' status would likely continue.

In a recent interview John stated:

> Social media has become a key part of my leadership strategy... Our lawyers said it was a terrible idea for me to tweet, but I ignored them. It's not unusual for one of my tweets to get 150 million impressions. This is no game. It's a way of driving my business.

You only have to tune in for a few minutes to understand that here is a man who not only 'gets' social, but he loves it. He balances the personal conversations with customers and team and showcases what he himself finds interesting or not, with the business performance side of things. His conversations take a very 'human' approach. One really feels as if one is getting a direct insight into his own values as well as the values of the business.

John agreed to be interviewed for the book, so you can hear directly about his objectives, tactics and advice. I wanted to interview him because whilst he is an extreme example of a social CEO, his values and purpose are very clear. Very simply, it is about engaging and serving the customer.

My favourite quote from John: 'Social can be one of THE most powerful tools in a CEO's toolbox today – if they'd just be open to it.'

Caron Bradshaw, CEO, Charity Finance Group (CFG)

I came across a piece of work Caron had shared via Twitter. It focused largely around leadership and referenced the importance of embracing new skills, which of course included social media. When I clicked to find out a little more about who was sharing the piece, it became obvious, as it often does on social media, that Caron and I had a number of common connections. A quick introduction tweet to say hello and explain what I was up to led to Caron happily agreeing to share her insights around social media and leadership.

As you will read in Caron's full interview, she is using social media to tune in to her landscape, as well as to network, thank and acknowledge people and connect. She also is sharing an informed voice about the sector she is passionate about.

My favourite quote from Caron: 'Authentic leadership requires vulnerability. We're human and should not be scared to show up and be seen.'

Kevin Burrowes, Head of Clients and Markets, PwC

Kevin is a partner in PwC's consulting business. He sits on the UK Executive Board with responsibility for clients and markets. He is also the Global Relationship Partner for a global bank.

I met Kevin around four years ago, when myself and David Taylor, co-author of my previous book, *The Business of Being Social*, were invited to talk to around 40 of Kevin's leadership team. Kevin had stumbled across our book and was championing social media within the team. At the time, a number of developments were happening within PwC regarding internal social networks, and so I was keen to interview Kevin to catch up on his view on social media and adoption within the organization.

My favourite quote from Kevin: 'Staying connected in a way that just wasn't possible 15 years ago is amazing. I've got friends and colleagues around the world and I can check in with them in an instant.'

Gordon Beattie, President and Founder, Beattie Communications

Gordon Beattie heads up a booming PR and marketing business.

A good friend of mine in the PR world mentioned to me that she had been to a talk where she had heard Gordon Beattie extolling the many benefits of social media. 'Gordon loves social media, you should interview him for your book', was her suggestion, and so I made contact with Gordon via LinkedIn and he kindly agreed.

In Gordon's interview, as well as sharing how he personally uses social media he also touches on the time commitment his organization gives to social media and content creation, and the business development opportunities it has realized.

My favourite quote from Gordon: 'If leaders turn their back on social, they are neglecting a fabulous opportunity to communicate with customers, employees and investors.'

Dr Sam Collins, author and CEO at Aspire

A chance Twitter discussion led me to Sam Collins, and it wasn't long before I realized that the person I was talking to on Twitter was also the author of a book I'd enjoyed. Having stayed connected with Sam and Aspire's activity via Twitter, Sam was a natural 'social CEO' for me to interview.

You will see from Sam's interview that as well as the big role that social media plays within her business, she cites the use of social media in helping to reach people and support campaigns relating to Aspire's foundation, all around the world. Without social media, she would have no means of even knowing about their existence.

My favourite quote from Sam: 'I think that as leaders we need to be braver and social media gives us an opportunity to do that. I get that we need to be balanced, but at the same time as leaders I think it is so important to have a voice and to be able to be brave about that voice.'

Kevin Roberts, author and former CEO at Saatchi & Saatchi

As referenced in Chapter 1, Kevin's book, *64 Shots: Leadership in a crazy world*, talks about Technological Quotient (TQ) and technology being embedded in modern society and that today's leaders need TQ in life, just to compete. He has held a number of leadership positions, including CEO at creative powerhouse Saatchi's for over 17 years, and so I was keen to hear what Kevin had to say about his own social media activity, and his candid thoughts on where social media is heading and its implications for leaders.

Whilst Kevin is the first to admit that he is not a heavy user of many of the channels, he recognizes the impact they can have from a thought leadership perspective, assisting with extending the reach of important brand messaging.

My favourite quote from Kevin: 'When a crisis comes, your social presence is something to either lean back into or defend/attack from.'

Shaa Wasmund MBE, author and Founder of Shaa.Com

I was introduced to Shaa during her time as founder and CEO of Smarta, a business that grew to become one of the UK's leading online repositories of advice and support for start-ups and SMEs. Shaa is a three-times bestselling author and now leads her business, Shaa.com, providing practical advice, training, support and coaching for entrepreneurs. She has had an eclectic career. Born in the United States and raised in the UK, she studied at the London School of Economics before becoming the only female boxing promoter in the UK, representing World Champion Chris Eubank and working with the infamous Don King before starting her own PR company, helping grow the Dyson brand from around Sir James Dyson's kitchen table.

Not one to mince her words, Shaa is highly active on social media, and her business helps other entrepreneurs to understand how the tools can be used to help grow and develop their own profiles and, in turn, their businesses. It is this dependency on 'being social' that led me to ask Shaa to share her views on how important social media is for her and her business and what advice she would share with other leaders.

My favourite quote from Shaa: 'Leaders need to take the time to understand where their audiences are and tune in, listen and communicate what needs to be said.'

Brian J Dunn, former CEO, Best Buy

When the seed of the idea was germinating for *Get Social*, I started researching the leadership space for great examples. As cited earlier, it wasn't the simplest of endeavours, but there were a few names that were cited as pioneers in engaging with social media at the leadership level. Brian Dunn, CEO of Best Buy, was one such name. I was thrilled when I made contact with Brian (again, via Twitter) and he very generously agreed to share his views, experience and advice. As one of the earliest senior leaders to adopt social media to communicate and connect, Brian's interview offers a number of highly practical insights.

My favourite quote from Brian: 'It was and is part of my life. To me, saying you don't have the time is like saying communication doesn't fit into your schedule.'

Steve Tappin, CEO, Xinfu, CEO Coach and host of the BBC's CEO Guru

During my research, I came across the BBC business programme *CEO Guru*, a series of interviews with CEOs of the biggest and fastest-growing companies. Steve hosts those interviews, and he is also the author of bestselling book *The Secrets of CEOs*. Over the years, Steve has interviewed a significant number of CEOs (over 200!), and so I was very interested to hear his views on and around social media and its adoption in the leadership space.

In true modern-day communication channel style, our interview was done via LinkedIn's messenger. For this reason, the questions vary a little from others you will find in the Appendix, but even though it is a briefer interview, there are still some gems to take away.

My favourite quote from Steve: 'I think CEOs should have a regular game plan to cover the next four to six weeks but must also be ready to adapt to opportunities that arise.'

Summary of key findings

I have purposely endeavoured to draw insights from an eclectic pool of leaders. However, whilst their sectors and organizations and, no doubt, they themselves, differ significantly, you will find a number of commonalities peppered throughout their interviews.

Whilst I again encourage you to read the interviews in full, let's now drill into some of the key themes.

Start slowly and do one thing really well

Having got this far with the book, you are hopefully feeling positive about getting started with social media. Or perhaps you are wondering how on earth you are going to fit 'being social' into your already busy day.

Your 90-day plan of action will help you map out exactly 'how' to get started. As I outlined in your plan and throughout the book, getting started doesn't mean that you have to dive in and start activity across a multitude of channels.

The advice from the majority of those doing the doing is to focus on 'owning one channel at a time', 'starting slowly' and 'getting one channel working really well before moving on to other channels'. Without exception, the advice from those doing the doing was to focus on consistency and quality over quantity.

Once you find your rhythm with social media and get into the habit of curating and creating content, tuning in to the influencers, content and audiences, then you can look to potentially expand the channels you are using. But only if it makes sense to do so and is aligned with your objectives.

Going back to your 90-day plan, the first step is all about determining your 'why', and uncovering the fundamental purpose of 'getting social'. Just because other leaders are using every channel possible, this doesn't mean you need to do the same. Being social is a personal endeavour. You do what fits with you. Explore the tools, find the one or ones that make sense for you personally, then execute your activity consistently and effectively.

From a leadership perspective, mastering one or perhaps two channels is great advice.

Authenticity

Talking about social media being a personal endeavour, throughout the book I've talked about the importance of authenticity in building trust and connection. Therefore, it was really interesting to hear each leader, without exception, talk about the importance of being their 'authentic' self on social media.

There were slightly different takes on authenticity – from truly showing up as yourself and having direct interactions with customers, employees and other audiences, to authentically sharing the good news, and perhaps the not-so-good news. The interviewees all advocated being transparent with viewpoints and showcasing what the brand stands for – being yourself, using your words, sharing your voice. They also touched on the aspect of being brave and bold, having a view, not being afraid to show vulnerability or take a stand and share your position on matters that matter to you and your organization. They all conveyed the idea that it was important to humanize yourself and, in turn, humanize the brand or organization.

Of course, being open, honest, transparent and authentic builds trust. And we all know the value of trust.

Where support fits in

This was another aspect of authenticity, related to the importance of social media activity being executed directly by the leader. Again, without exception, each of the leaders were proud to state that they managed their social media activity themselves. They tuned in to what was happening, usually on a daily basis. If they tweeted, or blogged, then it was their words, their comments, their curation, their decision to share.

When it comes to day-to-day activity, 'do it yourself' was a key theme, and from an 'authentic' voice and perspective. I was delighted to hear this. That said, of course, leaders and CEOs have enough to be getting on with, leading and steering. I was encouraged to hear that the majority of leaders realized the importance of getting support with their activity.

There was a real mix of support identified, either by having regular accountability sessions with, say, a PA or someone within the social media team – to review how activity is going and planning social media activity in advance – or working with the internal communications teams in getting assistance with messaging and content development, be that thought leadership blog posts or articles, image design, video or curation. They also recommended working with teams to align with the organization's social campaigns and getting help with analysis, KPIs and metrics or general training, upskilling and optimization.

It makes sense for leaders to reach out and get support, freeing up even more time for you the leader to spend time, authentically, on the channels, keeping tuned in and communicating.

Tuning in to customers and employees

Talking of tuning in and communicating, understanding how customers and employees feel came out as one of the key ways leaders are using social media. When mapping out the findings from the interviews, I always scribble key points onto Post-it notes as I'm reading. I then stick all my notes on a wall and start moving things around into similar clusters.

The 'interacting with customers and employees' was by far the largest cluster! Meaning that throughout the interviews and, indeed, throughout the research findings highlighted in previous chapters, this aspect was a common thread for leaders.

Of course, it's not just the capacity to tune in to customers and hear what they are directly saying in order to, as Brian J Dunn so perfectly put it, 'get a temperature check' that is facilitated by social media – there is also the 'real world, real time' element to consider.

Conversations are happening all the time, and leaders can tune in and listen in real time to those conversations. They can join in those conversations in real time too. This really helps to personalize the customer or employee experience. A simple response from the CEO or senior leader to an employee or customer lets them know they are being heard. An impromptu message of thanks or recognition to an employee or business unit creates an element of surprise and, from the examples cited within the book, generates significant positivity and goodwill.

It is creating connection where there wouldn't necessarily be connection. After all, the essence of being social – is to connect.

Work–life integration

Turning now to the more practical 'doing' aspects, and the questions and insights around fitting social media activity into an already busy schedule, here are some insights from the interviewees on how to balance their work and life commitments and when to engage with social media.

The consensus largely focused around there not being any specific 'separate time' to do social, but rather, the leaders I interviewed, seemed to have integrated it into their daily lives. 'It's an integral part of my life, it's integrated, not separate' was a common theme.

Social media channels enable you to create your own personal news feed, allow you to 'see round corners'. Given that the pace of social media activity is fast and fluid, then it makes sense to hear that the leaders interviewed are using time when commuting, travelling or just general downtime to scroll the feed(s).

Using real-time social media channels for tuning in and staying current with what is being said by people, and in areas that are important to you (employees, colleagues, influencers, competitors, stakeholders, partners, news channels), is a productive use of your time. When relevant, it also gives you the opportunity to engage with or perhaps lead a conversation. For those who did mention specific amounts of time they allocated to 'being social', it varied from two hours a day to two hours a week.

The key is defining what works for you and how you can fit it in. As outlined in Chapter 7 and the 90-day plan, this is likely to differ for each individual. Whilst there are certain pointers as to the level of activity to generate more activity, there is no one formula. But what we do know is that to generate traction and engagement, there does need to be an element of consistency and, more importantly, significant amounts of authenticity.

This brings us back to being yourself on social media. Let's liken it to how you would communicate face to face with your colleagues generally during a working week. Largely, your focus would be on work, and the majority of conversations and output would focus on more 'professional' subject matters. They would constitute natural conversations you have every week in your role as leader.

However, there will be times throughout that week where you will chat with colleagues and mention your family, your friends, your hobby or somewhere you've been, or something you read or watched, or a situation that amused or riled you. In just the same way, to keep your social activity authentic, it is likely that whilst your focus will largely be about what you do in your role as leader, those same personal, human and everyday life interactions will blend naturally in your social media output.

Thought leadership

There is no doubt that the social media channels are really useful for the amplification of thought leadership. When I say that, I don't mean that you have to be writing long white papers, or heavy blog posts. A simple tweet sharing your view on something is still thought leadership.

Kevin Roberts referred to the posts he creates as being an extension of his advice and beliefs. He particularly mentions the importance of showcasing expertise. The channels enable not only a platform on which to publish content but, as importantly, the opportunity to build a following of influencers, thought leaders, stakeholders, partners, customers and employees, and prospective stakeholders, customers, employees and partners.

Your content may be brilliant, inspiring, educational and informative but, as we discussed in Chapter 4, the reason we create content is to generate emotional connection and engagement. We do it to share a message and for others to receive and connect with that message. The social media channels offer potential far-reaching, mass-amplifying platforms from which to do that.

From a platform of one to many, as well as sharing your message you may also learn something about or from those tuning in. Certain viewpoints may chime with the audience, others may not. You may receive feedback to challenge your view, to stretch your thinking or to simply validate your thinking by supporting your view.

The key to thought leadership is consistency around your why, your message and communication. It is not about overpublishing and putting stuff out there for the sake of saying something, but rather an extension of your knowledge, experience and expertise where and when relevant.

Remember the point that I've reiterated throughout previous chapters: the platforms and the technology enable you to target audiences and distribute content. However, the real value in being social is the building engagement and awareness and developing and strengthening relationships. Your social media activity is not purely about creating and delivering content, but rather to inspire creative and meaningful conversations about your brand or organization.

Getting behind the thought leadership piece is about answering a number of questions around the question 'How do I show up?' Who is this leader, what do they stand for, what does their company stand for, what value do they add, what's their viewpoint? What goes into social media is an outcome – an outcome of years of hands-on learning and experience.

The next generation

In the first chapters of the book we explored the social landscape and the demographics of those using the channels.

There is no escaping the fact that millennials are already changing the workforce. As cited by Kevin Burrowes:

> Social is just a way of life for millennials who are moving into more and more senior management positions. We've got to keep up!

Dr Sam Collins shared:

> A whole new generation of people who grew up with social and for whom being social isn't anything unusual will become the bulk of the workforce. It's not going to be a nice-to-have any more.
>
> Those who don't have knowledge of and a good use of social media will fall behind.

Remember, the stats predict that by 2030 millennials will be approximately 75 per cent of the workforce (Holmes Noble, 2017).

From a leadership perspective, it makes sense to embrace and learn about the technologies and practices now, reap the benefits and put into place strong foundations for future leaders – and indeed, lead from the front in creating a social business.

In fact, when asked the question as to what piece of advice you would offer to other leaders or CEOs, the responses largely focused around the fact that social media is only going to continue to grow and evolve. It's not a fad, and it's certainly not going away. It's a necessary skill or competency that leaders need to embrace. It's a key component of progressive leadership.

And finally... getting started

Before we finish this chapter, another key theme cited focused around one of the most challenging aspects of getting social. That is, actually getting started.

My intention is that the 90-day plan, which is based around my Smart Social Focus Model (Plan, Listen, Analyse, Engage, Measure), really does provide you with a very implementable roadmap.

Like any project or new endeavour you embark on, it is always a little more challenging at the outset. It's new and it may not feel like the easiest thing to make time for. We are unlikely to remember learning to walk – but having watched my children, I have seen first-hand the frustration in mastering the technique. Now, it's natural. In my previous book, I likened getting started to a plane taking off. It expends the most fuel and energy at the outset on take-off – and then once it's in the air, it's pretty much plain sailing. Whichever analogy works for you, the message is that yes, there will be some effort and learning required at the outset. But in a relatively short time, it will become business as usual.

Reference

Holmes Noble (2017) [accessed 30 November 2017] The DNA of a Modern CEO [Online] https://www.holmesnoble.com/wp-content/uploads/2017/08/Holmes-Noble-The-DNA-of-a-modern-CEO.pdf

Afterword

And so here we are at the end of *Get Social*. Thank you for letting me hold your attention throughout the chapters.

My intention when setting out was very simple and hopefully very clear: to provide you with the stats and facts about the landscape, but more importantly, to equip you with the reasons it makes sense for you, a leader or aspiring leader, to 'get social' and then to provide you with a step-by-step roadmap for practical implementation.

Understanding is one thing. Doing is another.

I purposely haven't given you every step to setting up your social media accounts, as that's not what this book is about. But I will be providing lots of practical resources to make those aspects as simple as possible for you, via the www.getsocial.site. You are invited to jump in and access all that you need.

Over my years of consulting, I have learnt that the best way to help you to get started is to give you what you need right now. Not everything you could ever need. But what you need right now. It was important to me to cut through and down on both noise and the overwhelming amount of information out there. Hence why my simple and highly realistic 90-day plan features in this book.

For all of us, the world has changed. Call it a paradigm shift, or man's natural endeavours for progression. Our workplaces are changing, roles within our workplaces are changing, leadership within our workplaces is adapting – and importantly, the channels used for communication are changing.

The fundamental human needs around connection and communication, however, have not changed. Being open, honest, transparent and authentic builds trust. And we all know the value of trust.

Jay Baer, bestselling author and marketer, recently shared a tweet, which I have pinned as a favourite: 'Trust is the filter through which all business success must pass' (Baer, 2015).

Personally, I would go a stage further, integrating business and personal to state that: 'Trust is the filter through which all success must pass.'

Reference

Baer, Jay (2015) [accessed 30 November 2017] Trust is the Filter Through Which All Business Success Must Pass, *Twitter*, 2 April [Online] Twitter.com

APPENDIX
Interviews

John Legere, CEO, T-Mobile

You're the CEO of T-Mobile – and have got to be one of the most socially engaged leaders. You also recently said: 'It's not unusual for one of my tweets to get 150 million impressions. This is no game. It's a way of driving my business.' Can you explain what you mean by social media being a way of driving your business?

I mean that every leader out there needs to learn and understand the power of social media. These are real people, real customers and prospective customers – and they are giving real feedback that informs our business decisions. Anyone who doesn't see that is missing a huge opportunity.

Social has become a key driver of the Un-carrier revolution and a major part of my leadership strategy – on many levels. It has taken off beyond my expectations. I have more than 5.3 million Twitter followers. And I've jumped into other platforms – Facebook, Instagram and Periscope. Social is where I learn, it's where I get a ton of insight that helps me run T-Mobile. It's where my customers are and it's the first place they usually go to complain or compliment us. I want to see all of it – the good and the bad. No filters! By staying directly connected to our customers, I can drive the business forward and adapt more quickly to what customers need and want.

Think about it. You don't see the other guys engaging with their customers on social. Why? Are they afraid of hearing what their customers really think? Being on social allows for real-time, unfiltered feedback from my customers and employees. People are always asking where we get the ideas for our Un-carrier moves. I tell them to watch my Twitter feed. A great example is the launch of T-Mobile ONE. The number one request from customers on social was to end data limits. I heard them. And so we led the change and went all in on unlimited.

I've never met you, but from your tweets and social activity I feel like I've got a good understanding of who you are and what you stand for. What has driven you to be so outwardly 'authentic' in your social media activity?

What's the point of being on social if you are not going to be yourself? I'm the same person on social that I am running through Central Park. Just watch some of my Periscopes! Part of what I love about social is that it's a conversation. It's not just about broadcasting stuff at people. It has to be a real two-way discussion. So, when people give you feedback, you show them you've heard them by doing something about it.

I'm also a big believer in changing it up to keep things fresh. When I started Slow Cooker Sunday on Facebook Live, I knew it was a crazy thing for a CEO to do. But I like to put myself out there and share my passions – and you'll notice I even get some T-Mobile news in there. Over 1 million people now watch it each week. I had zero clue so many people would tune in. I've had a blast doing it. But, more importantly, it gives me a whole new way to connect with people AND share the T-Mobile story.

From running in the rain – to sharing your slow cooker recipes – whatever you are up to, you seamlessly integrate the personal/work aspect within your social activity. Is this something you consciously set out to do – or has your social activity evolved… can you share a little about how it's become what it is today?

Things have definitely evolved for me. How I share on social has changed as social platforms have changed. Right now, I love Instagram Stories, Facebook Live, Periscope (live Twitter streaming) – video in general – really anything that I can do live! I've learnt a lot along the way. My first Slow Cooker Sunday was filmed entirely sideways. Whoops. But it keeps things real. With me, what you see is what you get and I embrace it. I can connect with customers and employees from anywhere – no matter what I'm doing. I might be taking selfies with employees at a call centre, riding around on my Segway at Headquarters or getting ready behind the scenes for our next Un-carrier event… You never know what you'll find me doing in social.

How does your personal social media activity complement T-Mobile's brand and campaign activity?

Besides being a walking advertisement? Just about every day, I'm telling people what T-Mobile is doing for them. I'm telling them about T-Mobile Tuesday giveaways, early access into concerts at T-Mobile Arena, amazing offers such as unlimited baseball with free MLB TV – everything I do on social is about what we're doing for our customers.

And, by the way, my social platform is just one part of the T-Mobile brand and how we engage with customers. Our social dominance as a brand gives us an outsized voice in this industry and helps us punch above our weight. We reach more people on social than our competitors Dumb and Dumber (Verizon and AT&T), whose market caps are at least five times our size.

We also do a ton of customer support in social. Our T-Force organization is working 24/7 real time via Twitter and other channels to help customers solve any issues they have. For example, on social, customers want to know they are dealing with a real person, so we launched custom profiles on Twitter. No more uncertainty – you know that you are chatting with a live person through DMs and not a chat bot. We were also the first company to launch asynchronous messaging with customers, so they can communicate with their Care rep in a time frame that works for them. And that's just a glimpse of what we've got coming!

I've said it before and I'll say it again... Social is a huge opportunity for businesses to reach consumers, share their stories, learn what their customers want and support their customers' needs. If you are not afraid of it, it is a fantastic addition to any business!

When I contacted you via Twitter to ask if I could feature you in my book – you quickly came back to me. I note that you do the same with questions – and gripes – you're very hands on with the two-way conversation. Some people would say corresponding with people on Twitter and other networks is not a CEO's job. What's your view on CEOs/leaders leading from the front and being accessible to their audiences?

People who say a CEO shouldn't be on Twitter just don't get it. I'd venture to guess they are not super connected with their customers either. Social has changed the rules of the game. It's real-time. It's open and transparent. People want to do business with companies that embrace this. They don't want a suit for a CEO that sits in boardrooms all day. Social can be one of THE most powerful tools in a CEO's toolbox today – if they would just be open to it. When it comes to social, I live by three core principles:

1 Listen

A big difference between other CEOs and me is that I spend more of my time listening.

2 Engage

Whether I'm helping customers, urging the other guys' customers to switch, or calling out the competition on their BS, I'm constantly engaging. A lot of CEOs seem to be on social to broadcast their opinions. What a waste. About 40 per cent of my tweets are replies. I love the conversation.

3 Have fun

I'm having a blast on social. Did you see my face-swap with DJ Khaled on Snapchat! And I love doing Slow Cooker Sunday. I laugh a lot and learn something new every day.

Most importantly – keep it real. Customers want a real conversation, not a curated interaction. And you've got to be prepared to take the good with the bad. Any CEO who is not actively engaging with their customers and employees on social is missing a huge opportunity.

One key objection for embracing social cited by CEOs is finding the time – what is your view on that?

The seismic changes we're living through demand that leaders change. I make time for social. The fact that I can do it from anywhere, any time on mobile makes it far easier to make time. Having seen the impact of social on my business, I have no intention of slowing down. In today's world, not to put these tools to use would be a dereliction of duty. Social allows us to stay connected to our customers and employees in ways that simply were not possible before. I'm frankly blown away that more CEOs don't make more time for it.

Another key objection cited is 'fear' – the fear of publicly saying the wrong thing. Given that you are often bold, what's your view on this objection?

In my experience, the more willing you are to take risks and be real, the more people are likely to follow you and believe in you. Our customers deserve that. I'm willing to go there.

Do today's CEOs need to adapt quickly to social media? Adapt or die. What's your view?

Any CEO who is not actively engaging with customers and employees on social is missing the boat. Beyond that, it's a disservice to your customers if you're not willing to be out there talking with them directly. People want to do business with companies they feel are open and that they can trust. For those willing to put themselves out there, who can take criticism, who can take the good with the bad – there's a ton of upside to be had.

On the practical side, you make everything seem so effortless and natural – what planning efforts, if any, go into your social media and content creaion to align with key campaigns?

It looks natural because it is. What you see is what you get. I do get some help with bigger initiatives and content creation – like video and sometimes contest ideas etc – but I do the day-to-day social myself.

How much time would you say you dedicate to social media activity? Are you supported by a social media team/assistant/agency?

I'm actively involved with all my social accounts every day 24/7 – I've just folded it into everything I do. Of course, if we have big launches going on, I do get some help from my team, but no agency support, no bots. What you see is all me and while it can be crazy hard to keep up with it – it's worth the effort!

I recall reading how your communication style has empowered team members within T-Mobile to be more social. What lessons do you have to share with others as to how you have structured social media within your business?

I've encouraged my entire leadership team to be on social. They need to be connected to our customers, too. In general, I encourage them to listen, engage and react. Just putting stuff out there and walking away is not what social is about.

Are there any particular stories/moments that really stand out for you – that showcase just how powerful social media has been for you and your business?

There are too many to recount. I've had people reading my live tweets during live TV broadcasts. Crazy. And I'm still blown away when I see tweets from people switching to T-Mobile because of something I said or did on social. People just want to be heard. And, when they are, they're moved. Their perceptions change, which is powerful. It's those moments I love most.

Do you have anything to share regarding the ability to tune into others, track conversations and listen to audience sentiment on social media?

First, I can't emphasize enough the importance of listening. That's still too rare in business. And don't simply listen to what customers are saying about your business. Listen to what people are saying to your competitors. In my industry, I've found that's a great way of learning what *not* to do.

As a CEO, leader and person, what is the most challenging aspect of 'being social'?

Putting yourself out there means opening yourself to raw emotion, opinions and criticisms. I sometimes hear from customers who have a problem that is frustrating them. That's never easy to hear. But I'm always grateful that they're willing to reach out to me directly. And I always engage and follow up. Being super connected with customers allows me to far more easily and quickly address their issues or pain points.

What is the most rewarding aspect of 'being social'?

Not to pick too much on the other guys, but they really do suck at social. We made a decision to be a totally different kind of wireless company – an Un-carrier – by actually listening to our customers and giving them the wireless experience they wanted. Social has played a huge role in this. And it's working. We've literally gone from America's fastest *shrinking* wireless company to America's fastest *growing* wireless company. Over 1 million customers have switched to T-Mobile every quarter for the past 17 quarters. Today, we have more than 70 million happy customers.

None of that would have been possible without all the followers, employees, reporters, colleagues and even critics who have been vocal in social, sharing their feedback, ideas, questions and comments. To all these people, I say, 'Thank you. Let's keep talking.'

What is the outlook for the next 10 years – where are we heading with social?

The democratization of content is here. Social is obviously central to this. And, of course, content is going mobile as the internet goes mobile. We are all consuming and creating content everywhere all the time. These are trends that are absolutely going to continue and eventually take over completely.

And this doesn't even begin to touch on the new social technologies and platforms that are going to become possible in a 5G world. The possibilities for VR, AR and entirely new experiences in the social space are enormous. I can't wait.

In true 'John Legere' style – what words of advice would you give to other CEOs?

Tune in to those you trust. Listen to your employees. Listen to your customers. Shut the f$&# up and do what they tell you.

Life is short. Don't forget to have fun. And, of course, always be yourself. This world needs more real people.

Caron Bradshaw, CEO, Charity Finance Group (CFG)

As the CEO of Charity Finance Group (CFG), what role does social media play in your working life?

Pretty much the first thing I do (whilst eating breakfast) in the morning is check social media: Twitter, LinkedIn, Facebook and Instagram. It's not something that I obsess about or pore over in great detail – just a brief check through, like looking at the morning papers used to be. It's the way I get a feel for the mood out there. It allows me to pick up things quickly – who is moving, what reports have been released, what stories have hit the press and so on. When I get to work I will also periodically check in on social media through the day. Again, not spending hours but quick check-ins (much as I would my emails).

It plays a powerful part in giving me easy-to-digest updates and quick connections with my stakeholders, colleagues, the wider sector (and sectors). It helps me feel connected and informed. So the short answer is, it plays an increasingly important part of my working life.

How does your personal social media activity complement CFG's brand and campaign activity?

I perceive that social media is as much about the 'social' as it is about the 'media'. Thus, I am not afraid to show myself. That is not to say that I will talk about anything and everything – there are limits to what I feel would be appropriate to share (and topics where CFG have deliberately not taken a stance where it would be unhelpful to comment or engage too heavily). The relationships that you can form from social media connections are important and it is unlikely that a cold, broadcasting or dictating approach would engage with people who I have not, and may never, meet. It would also not be the authentic me. I like to chat, I have a creative mind and I feel relationships are very important. By showing myself authentically I hope that this reinforces what CFG is striving to be. I hope it strengthens our brand and promotes a positive image of CFG.

Some would say corresponding with people on social media is not what CEOs should be doing. What's your view?

I think that is a very 'traditional' view of what being a CEO is. Progressive leadership requires you to be present, available, connected, visible and authentic. It also requires, in my view, vulnerability. Not all CEOs are comfortable being vulnerable – putting themselves out there to people in a less 'controlled' way. That's okay if that is the type of CEO you are and want to be. Who am I to judge whether that's right? It just is not the type of leader I wish to be. However, I would never encourage CEOs to fudge it – to be on social media in name and have others tweet/blog or share posts for you. Equally, trying to force a persona that you think people will like can be seen through so quickly. If you're out there, you have to be authentic.

What about the practicalities of being social – what advice can you share about content creation/curation and day-to-day activity?

A lot of people I've spoken to (particularly those who are not big social media users) are scared about the risks associated with putting out content that hasn't gone through a rigorous process and scrutiny. I see it more as an extension to less formal communications that you might have, say, at a networking event. You use judgement on what to share and what not to say, you engage in positive conversations and walk away from those that are going nowhere – and you definitely don't hit the wine! Of course, when you put something out there in writing it does have a greater level of permanence.

I don't tend to worry too much about silly typos or getting something wrong innocently. It's easy to laugh at your own typos or to correct misunderstandings provided that you are not reckless. On the other side it is too easy to allow social media to take over without it being a valuable or meaningful addition to your work so I would caution people about spending too much time trying to respond to everything.

I think that the balance in what you say is important; too much 'here is what my work is doing' can feel like a salesperson touting for business (not in itself a bad thing but I don't think helpful to a CEO). Conversely, too much personal stuff or opinion can narrow your network rather than expand it.

Finally, I would encourage people to show up – to be themselves and give it a go. Don't let someone else do it for you (people will see through it); try a little at first and see where it takes you. It's not about the volume of followers you have (though clearly the broader the network the greater the potential pool of people to engage with), it is more about the quality of the conversations your social media presence can lead to.

Which social channels do you use and why?

For work I use Twitter, Instagram and LinkedIn. I also use our blog and do guest blogs for others from time to time. (CFG also has a small charity Facebook page – but I don't engage with that through Facebook because my Facebook page is for personal use.) I limit how I engage with my children on Twitter or Instagram because I want to limit the exposure they have on their own social media presence (but I am not averse to posting pictures of them).

For personal use I have Facebook (and I use Instagram, Twitter and LinkedIn to an extent in a personal way too, as outlined above). I make a few connections through work that I become more 'friends' with than work colleagues and I do have a smattering of those people on my Facebook group. This has been helpful for work and has led to sourcing a few speakers, articles and raffle prizes! But I try to keep Facebook more narrowly focused on my friends and family.

How much time would you say you dedicate to social media activity?

When you add it all together I guess about an hour or two a day. I tend to do quite a bit of catching up in my time (breakfast, train journey, over lunch), but that is more to do with meetings and available time rather than seeing it as something separate to work.

What's your view on CEOs needing to adapt quickly to social media?

To me the increasing importance of being you and the pace of business both mean that failure to engage with social media may leave you behind. The generation of workers we are employing and engaging with were brought up with social media as an integral part of their networking and communications – Snapchatting, WhatsApping and other 'inging' that I don't currently use that actively. It feels rather luddite to refuse to engage – a bit like sticking to fax when email came in!

Do you plan your social media and content creation?

CFG's content is definitely planned. I will of course tweet or share links to advance that content. However, this is less choreographed.

I wouldn't say that my social media use is chaotic or unstructured though. The best analogy I could give comes from the world of 'improv'; freedom within structure (noticing more, using everything and letting go). I guess my social media is 'improv'!

Are you supported by a social media team/assistant/agency?

We have a comms team and they will help me by creating short-form content for online content or discussing difficult topics that I might be unsure whether it would be sensible to engage with. However, what I share is down to me and my judgement. I may also have blogs part-drafted or structured for me for expedience, but I write most of my own content (either entirely or mostly). It is important that my words have my voice.

Many CEOs/leaders cite 'fear of saying the wrong thing' as a barrier to getting on social – what are your views around that?

You might! But as long as you use your judgement and you are not reckless in what you say. Following these three rules might help: never tweet if you're very angry, have drunk too much, or are overly tired. As I said before – to me this is authentic leadership, it requires vulnerability. We're human and should not be scared to show up and be seen.

Another key barrier to getting social is 'time' – not having the time to build social properly into the work–life schedule. What are your views on this?

Time can be tight and so the important thing is to ensure you don't let it rule your life. Setting aside time each day for a social media catch-up is a good habit to form. It means that you have a more consistent presence and can form relationships more easily. If you just pop up every so often to promote your work then disappear again, people will switch off. They get too many adverts already!

As a busy CEO/leader, what is the most challenging aspect of 'being social'?

I have an opinion on everything (or most things anyway) – so sometimes resisting the urge to say something when it would be unwise to do so can be a challenge. However, I just picture myself in a telephone conversation with a journalist and ask whether it would be in my or my organization's interests to see what I want to say as a headline. If the answer is no, then I don't say it.

What is the most rewarding aspect of 'being social'?

The relationships you can build. I have met several people virtually first and then in person. From some of those connections I have gained staff. Other connections have been mutually rewarding and have helped me to keep my finger on the pulse.

Do you have any specific stories/examples of where social has really proved beneficial for you? Assisting you and your business directly?

A few years back I sat on a train talking with a colleague about what we do. A young man overheard the conversation and told me that he was working in that area. I didn't have his contact details but I remembered his name. We connected via Twitter and he ended up speaking at our main annual conference about his experience and the power of social media!

What's the outlook for the next 10 years – where are we heading with social media?

Gosh, I am no techno predictor but I think that we will see increased use of online and socially driven content. People can get immediate information and answers using social media (which has great potential for a service industry such as charity). I understand that a big thing on the horizon is the advancements in artificial intelligence and this has both opportunities and risk (as with all things). I suspect that in 10 years' time we will look back on 'social media' as a quaint term for the way we simply do business!

What words of advice would you give other CEOs/leaders…?

Do it. Be authentic. Speak with your voice. Don't overthink it but don't be reckless.

Kevin Burrowes, Head of Clients and Markets, PwC

(Kevin sits on the UK Executive Board with responsibility for clients and markets. He is also the Global Relationship Partner for a global bank.)

Why do you use social media – what is social media for you?

I use social media because I enjoy it. I think it is a great and easy way to connect with people, increase your knowledge and keep on top of business issues in real time. This is particularly important for me as a leader of PwC, an organization that prides itself on being able to solve our clients' challenges. I need to keep up to speed with the opportunities and issues that face our clients so that I can work with them and advise them, and social media is a great way to do this.

From a personal perspective, it's a fantastic way of building my brand. It also helps me to be more accessible and human to both my clients and people within PwC, which is important to me.

Since we met almost three years ago, have you seen any change of attitude towards social media at the more senior level?

Yes, I definitely think that attitudes towards social media have changed. More and more senior people have social media accounts and are communicating through digital channels. I also think that more people now understand and see the value in social media, whereas three years ago many still viewed it with suspicion and were perhaps somewhat nervous about engaging with it.

That being said, I think we still have some way to go in terms of senior business leaders regularly using social media, but I'm sure this will continue to increase over the next three years! Technology is moving fast and I really passionately believe that embracing technology is critical whatever age you are or whatever business you're in.

When we last met you spoke about the work PwC is doing to introduce more collaboration tools across the business. How is this going and what impact has it had to date?

The way we work is changing with new technologies and demands from our workforce and as a firm we've got to keep up with the pace of change. One of the ways that we're trying to disrupt ourselves is by adopting the latest, world-leading technologies such as Salesforce and Google at work. Both of these tools are fantastic for collaboration, and we've got to now ensure that we have the right mindset and behaviours to really make the most of them in the long term.

It's a journey, but we are already seeing people come together from different parts of the business, different regions and even different countries in a way that they hadn't before to share knowledge and create even better outputs for our clients. It's really exciting for me and I'm looking forward to seeing where we'll go next with this.

How is social media activity encouraged and managed within PwC?

At PwC, we encourage our people to use social media to connect with clients and targets, share thought leadership and build their own and the PwC brand. There are two strands of training. First, we provide social media masterclasses and e-learns. These are great for learning about the different channel options and best-practice methods for sharing the firm's thought leadership, views and ideas.

We also have a reverse mentoring programme, which has been running for four years now. Through this, our partners and directors spend time with our junior members of staff to learn about how to best deploy social media tools and channels to build their personal brand and to connect with our clients and stakeholders. Over half of the partnership have been through this programme, including myself!

Monitoring and managing our social media presence is also really important for us, and we have a central team that does this. We use monitoring tools to alert us to potential issues and opportunities and also to measure our collective impact in the market.

How much time would you say, on average, do you spend on social media activity? Do you have a fixed pattern? How does it fit into your everyday working life?

I'd say that there are three layers to this.

Every day I check social media, especially Twitter, to keep up to date with the latest news and business stories. I'll share or retweet anything that is relevant to my followers and the profile that I'm building. We also have a central content and media site at PwC where I can see all of the main PwC messages and personalize and share any that are relevant.

Then, there's my ad hoc activity. This is mainly sharing pictures or key discussion points from events I'm attending or speaking at. To be honest, I really don't do as much of this as I should. I get to meet so many interesting people and go to some great events and I need to get into the habit of sharing this more on social media!

Finally, each month I sit down with my PA to go through what I have done and what else I could be doing to keep improving my social media profile. For example, we look at whether anything needs to be done to maintain my All-Star status on LinkedIn and how I'm doing in the internal PwC social media rankings. My goal is to get into the top 10, but I think I'm about 40th at the moment so I've still got some improvements to make!

What's your view around leaders needing to adapt quickly to social?

I honestly think that business leaders who are not using social media are missing out. It's a really powerful way to engage with people, both inside and outside of your company, keep up to date with what's going on and also get your own messages across. It's a great way to get your brand across and can really impact how you're seen in the marketplace.

For example, when I have business meetings, especially with some-one I've never met before, I often look at Google and Salesforce to find out more about that person. Social media profiles come up top of the search every time. For this reason alone it's so important to make sure your profiles are up to date... it could be a bad first impression if not! Having an out-of-date LinkedIn profile or empty Twitter feed really doesn't look good.

I also think that leaders who don't engage with social risk being left behind. Social media is a just a way of life for many millennials who are moving into more and more senior management positions. We've got to keep up!

What would you say is your most challenging aspect of being social?

Getting the balance right between being personal and corporate can sometimes be a challenge. I often see people on Twitter having a rant about something frustrating that has happened, but it wouldn't be professional for me to do that in my role and could have some serious implications.

You've always got to think about what you're saying and what the impact of that could be. Remember too that old posts are stored and available for anyone to see if your profiles are open; there's been several examples in the news recently where people have been caught out with inappropriate or unprofessional twitter posts from several years ago. My rule is: if you have even the slightest doubt about what you want to say, don't post it.

What's the most rewarding aspect of being social?

Staying connected in a way that just wasn't possible 15 years ago is amazing. I've got friends and colleagues around the world and I can check in with them in an instant. I can also keep up to date with what's going on around the world as most news stories are broken first on social media.

Also the ability to influence and get your views across on social media is phenomenal. Two of our PwC partners have over 50,000 Twitter followers each and they use that platform to promote diversity and inclusion, amongst other things, which I think is fantastic.

The influencer aspect is highly interesting, especially if the consumers – and by that I mean clients and organizations – are selecting who they do business with…

I think this comes back to what I've touched on earlier about using social media as a distribution channel to showcase your brand and what you stand for, and to build your reputation. This can be really powerful for both individuals and organizations. At PwC, we published our BAME pay gap in our recent annual report, which was interactive and digital for the first time ever. The conversation on social media around this reached 35 million people and was discussed by a number of influencers. Many organizations came to us off the back of that conversation to work with us on gender and BAME gap issues – not only because we had the best team, but because we had started the conversation and shown our commitment to these issues through that.

What words of advice would you give the other leaders, other CEOs who might be curious about getting into social?

Get involved and embrace it! If you don't know where to start, find someone who is experienced at it to help you with the dos and don'ts and show you how to get the best out of it. Social media is a fantastic tool and you're really missing out if you're not using it.

Dr Sam Collins, CEO, Aspire

What role does social media play for you in your working life?

It plays a pretty big role actually, and it has been growing and evolving over the past few years. Whereas originally it was more about networking and connecting, it then developed into a way of marketing and now it's much more about using social media to reach and engage with women all over the world, and also to connect with other campaigns around the world, which we would never ordinarily be able to know about or have access to if there wasn't such a thing as social media. The transition sounds quite linear, but it's not, because it still fulfils all of those roles at the same time.

Originally, as we were learning more about social media and trying to figure out how appropriate it was for our business and our charity, and also how much time it was going to take and whether we were doing it properly, it felt a little bit like a chore. Whereas now, we've realized that a key factor is the importance of enjoying it, because that comes across in our posts. Another key thing we learnt is that it has to have a strategy around it. If there isn't a strategy around it, it tends to get lost and doesn't work so well.

I think one of the biggest things I learnt was that, initially, I always felt it was important to be posting content: 'We should be posting, we should be posting, we should be posting, we should be posting', and I think a lot of people post, post, post, but the key to social media is actually about connecting with other people. Tuning in, listening.

Sharing other people's content, commenting and communication on the posts. That's how you start to make real connections.

As the CEO, how do you manage your social media activity from a personal perspective and balancing your viewpoint?

Social media provides a highly useful platform to showcase your brand, whether that's your personal brand or your organizational brand.

You still want to be your own personality as the CEO of your organization. It's about making sure that there is a strategy in place, for me as Dr Sam Collins, CEO of Aspire, and also a strategy in place for Aspire – and that both work in parallel.

I think that as leaders we need to be braver and social media gives us an opportunity to do that. I get that we need to be balanced, but at the same time, as leaders, I think it's so important to have a voice and to be able to be brave about that voice.

I saw an example recently that I thought was brilliant. Relating to Campbell's Soup and their 'Two Dads' campaign. You read all this backlash on Twitter, but I loved, loved, loved the social media response from Campbell's back to those negative comments. They weren't normal vanilla corporate, 'We're really sorry you're upset. Here's a can of Campbell's soup' responses, they basically said, 'We believe in this and if you don't like it, don't buy our soup.'

I wish there were more companies braver in taking a stand for what's right. The backward view out there is that it's not okay to be two dads. You have a voice as an organization and social media enables you to use it. I never even thought about buying Campbell's soup and now I'm buying Campbell's soup forever.

I think that everyone is realizing the power of social media. I mean, governments have been overturned because messages have gone around very quickly on Twitter.

Which channels are you active on and what does your day-to-day activity look like?

I'm active on Facebook, LinkedIn and Twitter mostly, and YouTube. My niece keeps bothering me about being on Snapchat and Instagram, but I haven't progressed that far yet. I post most days, and I schedule time into my daily plan to post, but those posts are aligned with the overall strategy of what Aspire's postings are about. I normally do posts in the morning, usually before I get the kids to school, because that's when I'm most awake and inspired. My formal posting is then done for the day. But I'm checking social media and tuning in probably every half an hour throughout the day, looking at what's going on and what people are posting.

If we've got a campaign going on or if I know that one of my friends or colleagues has an active campaign, I'll be looking to see what's going on there too. I often get asked to support campaigns, and asked to promote other events and conferences, and if it's something that I want to endorse and support, then I'll do that over social media.

Not having the time is often cited as a challenge for using social media, what are your views on that?

I think that women are natural connectors and we're naturally social. For women, everything flows around what we're doing. I might do 10 minutes on social before I take the kids to school, and then I may have a coaching session, and as I'm winding down for lunch, I'll spend some more time on social. I may spend a bit of time looking at it over lunch too. My activity on social doesn't feel like, 'Oh, now I've got to do my social media' – it's woven into the context of my day.

Social media is often quite light. It's easy to flip through social media. It's like flicking the channels on TV.

Therefore, the personal and professional side of social media for me flows and is all part of my activity. At the same time, I'm posting on our company page on Facebook and I'm checking to see what my sister's kids are doing with their new school uniforms.

You mentioned social is like flicking through TV channels. Do you find yourself turning to social media channels to keep up to date with what's happening, rather than traditional channels?

Most definitely and especially for emergencies. We had an event in March that was the day after the terrorist attack on Westminster, so the way that we were getting our information real-time the evening before the event was definitely through Twitter. However, you do have to be prepared to root through the rubbish before you really make sure that you're getting news from good sources. The real-time aspect of channels such as Twitter, I would say, in any kind of emergency situation, is really, really useful.

Do I turn to social in general for news and events? Probably not so much. I'm a bit more traditional. I still like the BBC, CNN, but that said, I think that will probably change as time goes on.

Looking forward then, what do you think the outlook for the next 10 years is with where we're heading with social?

For us it's still a thing that is separate from us. We still see it as something we need to do, something to learn about, especially as a senior leader, it's still like a new thing. We didn't grow up with it – whereas in the next 10 years, it'll be the norm. A whole new generation of people who grew up with social and for whom being social isn't anything unusual will become the bulk of the workforce. It's not going to be a nice-to-have any more.

Those who don't have knowledge of and a good use of social media will fall behind. I hope that's true, because there's also a theory that it all sort of might explode at some point because it's just too much, but I'm forever the optimist, so I think that the next generation is going to really show us how it's done, and it's only going to get better, faster, more efficient and more useful as the technology gets better.

One of the things I'm seeing and that I think is really quite amazing is when you go to a very poorly developed country where there is little food to eat, but people still have access to a phone and, in many circumstances, access to social media. Not all, because there's still a large part of the world that has no access to the internet, but you now see people with access to social media who would never have had access to social media before. I think that's really exciting. It's also a little scary in some circumstances when you think of what's going on in terms of radicalizing and recruiting people, but at the same time you start seeing women, particularly, who are able to communicate and gather in societies where they ordinarily would never have been able to do that without social media.

That's what I think is really terrific. In the next 10 years I can only see that aspect growing. And really the world is in a very poor state right now with regards to so many things, but you know, when you start seeing people doing good things and coming together doing good things, it's powerful and social media is a vehicle for that.

What advice would you give to other CEOs and leaders who are potentially wavering or still think it's a nonsense or don't have the time or are afraid? What would you say?

I would say start slowly and be brave and start to see the value of it and enjoy yourself. There's enough to do when you're a CEO without feeling like it's another thing on the list to tick off. Instead, use it as a way to connect. Particularly use it as a way to connect with other CEOs, because being a CEO can be a very lonely place. It's a great opportunity to meet other like-minded people if you're brave enough to do that and make those connections. Don't be scared of it. Be brave, be bold and go for it and see the value.

Gordon Beattie, CEO, Beattie Communications

As the CEO of Beattie Communications, what role does social media play in your working life?

It plays a key role for me and Beattie, the creative communications group. As a company we have won millions of pounds worth of new business via our social media sites. That's why we invest more than 40 hours every week creating social media content. I post updates every single day while spending at least 30 minutes of my time every day on social sites – primarily LinkedIn and Facebook.

How does your personal social media activity align with Beattie Communications' brand and campaign activity?

I have nearly 10,000 followers on Twitter and more than 3,300 on LinkedIn so my daily updates keep Beattie Group and Only Marketing front of mind.

What do you say to those who don't think CEOs should be corresponding with people on social media?

Balderdash – every CEO should be on social media. If it's good enough for the current and previous US Presidents, it's good enough for every CEO. If they turn their back on social they are neglecting a fabulous opportunity to communicate with customers, employees and investors.

Which social media channels do you use – and why?

Twitter because it's a great vehicle for sharing current news. LinkedIn because it's used by decision makers. Facebook as a selling tool. Snapchat to reach Generation Y.

What advice can you share about content creation/curation and day-to-day activity?

The secret is posting interesting, inspirational or arresting material each and every day. Use rich media including pictures and video – and be sure to listen!

Do you plan your own social media and content creation – or are you supported by a social media team/assistant/agency?

I do most of it myself but we have a dedicated social team serving clients.

How have you structured social media within your business(es)?

We encourage everyone in the company to be active on social media.

What's the most challenging aspect of 'being social'?

Nothing is challenging. It's as normal as breathing.

What's the most rewarding aspect of 'being social'?

The amount of sales leads it generates.

What's the outlook for the next 10 years – where are we heading with social?

More and more and more.

What words of advice would you give to other CEOs?

Take the shot.

Kevin Roberts, CEO, Redrose Consulting

Kevin, across your previous and current roles, what role has/does social media play in your working life?

I've blogged for a decade, creating something like 2,000 posts. KR Connect has been a publishing and broadcast medium for experimenting with ideas, riffing on stuff I like and love, expanding on themes and topics from my books on leadership and Lovemarks.

For me, LinkedIn is a new and relatively useful way of engaging with a professional cohort. I have a Twitter account but I don't love the medium. It's too superficial for me. I have never Facebooked. I prefer my personal privacy.

How does your personal social media activity blend with your professional activity?

It's a professional/personal blend, akin to work–life integration: thought leadership, and interesting fodder I come across, personal interests such as great music, rugby (the game they play in heaven), compelling television, memorable hotels, all connected by an idea… the currency of our generation.

Some would say corresponding with people on social media is not what CEOs/leaders should be spending their time doing. What's your view?

I generally agree. CEOs and leaders should monitor and read social media about their companies – and focus on running their companies. CEOs are not politicians or celebrities, they have serious work to do. Companies need social media channels related to the business or serving customers. In politics and showbusiness there are no lines of decorum; in business there are (or should be!). This doesn't deny the role social media has in business, it simply says that the number one job of companies is to delight customers with the products and services they make and sell, and not to get into stupid fights on Twitter. Social media needs to be in the service of your company and your customers.

What about the practicalities of being social – what advice can you share about content creation/curation and day-to-day activity?

Have a consistent flow of content. Not constant, but a consistent cadence that audiences come to expect and anticipate. Don't over-publish. Select one medium and do it really well.

Content should be an outcome of your natural curiosity about what makes the world go round. Always offer something interesting.

Get assistance, whether it's research or the actual act of publishing. As a CEO you have so little time, so don't be self-righteous about doing everything.

How much time would you say you dedicate to social media activity?

Two hours a week. Be disciplined. Prioritize running the business over putting out a post.

What's your view about today's CEOs needing to adapt quickly to social?

This is and has always been true. Since people learnt to communicate and live with others, leaders need to adapt to communicate effectively. The technology may have changed, but the need hasn't.

Do you plan your social media and content creation?

Yes... I start with the two i's, the common theme, ideas and inspiration. I am a radical optimist and my content is always upbeat. There's enough criticism and negative commentary in the world without adding to the doom and gloom. I prefer sunshine. Some posts relate to current events, some come from articles that I've saved from the weekend papers, or a note scribbled in the margin after someone has said something revelatory in a meeting. Curiosity must be the driver, and when you are curious you are always searching, storing, curating.

Are you supported by a social media team/assistant/agency?

Yes.

Many CEOs/leaders cite 'fear of saying the wrong thing' as a barrier to getting on social – what are your views around that?

Politicians and celebrities can say and do anything and it is accepted behaviour. Businesses have shareholders and customers, and operate in an entirely different paradigm of accountability. Fear should never be a driver – you can't be a leader or CEO if you're held back by fear. As General Norman Schwarzkopf said, 'When given command, take charge and do what's right.'

Another key barrier to getting social is 'time' – not having the time to build social properly into the work–life schedule. What are your views on this?

It's about work–life integration. Make happy choices. Follow your heart. Work hard, have fun. As Coco Chanel said, 'There's time for work and time for love. That leaves no other time.'

As a busy CEO/leader, what's the most challenging aspect of 'being social'?

Responding. I switched off the comments section of my blog because it was simply too time-consuming to respond, argue, defend, engage. As I have said, I view social, in my case, blogging, as a broadcast, mono-directional distribution medium. If people are motivated to write to me thoughtfully, I always give them the respect of a reply – with my pen.

What's the most rewarding aspect of 'being social'?

Assembling a coherency of thought over a decade and more. A lot of social is hot air, gone the millisecond it is published. I've posted a body of work that I am proud of.

Do you have any specific stories/examples of where social has really proved beneficial for you, assisting you and your business directly?

I was in the advertising business for 20 years; clients came to us for thought leadership and it was important to show we had some! Social has been very useful in this regard. At Saatchi & Saatchi I published or commissioned or supported the publication of over a dozen books; all of them served a specific strategic purpose. Books last for ever, and they take ages to make. For me, social is a real-time extension of these books: extending themes, building on material and arguments, being a library for valuable material I've rambled and rumbled across.

What's the outlook for the next 10 years – where are we heading with social?

The brilliant media professor at NYU Neil Postman wrote a book about television called *Amusing Ourselves to Death*. He could have written it about social media. I don't really care where the technology goes, it will be more instant, granulated and compressed. I do care about focus and attention spans, and social media can become a weapon of mass distraction; a massive time suck and energy sapper.

What words of advice would you give other CEOs/leaders?

Understand and practise the mediums in the context of your customers and your company. Have a social presence somewhere on the spectrum, and execute it consistently.

When a crisis comes, your social presence is something to either lean back into or defend/attack from. If you want an unfettered platform, go into politics or showbusiness.

Please feel free to share any other views/aspects/insights

Start by doing one thing and doing it really well. Pay attention but don't get distracted. Use social to be expressive, creative and inspirational. Get savvy support for finessing your content and for astutely building an audience.

Shaa Wasmund, CEO, Shaa.com

As former founder and CEO of Smarta, exec on a number of boards and now CEO of Shaa.com, what role has/does social media play in your working life?

Oh my goodness, huge! Without platforms like Facebook there's no way we could have built the amazing tribe of people we have supporting us every day. It's such a great way to target and reach our ideal customer base. It also allows us to regularly share content and have direct conversations to show them exactly what we and our brand stand for and why we love what we do.

How does your personal social media activity blend with your professional activity?

The work I do is part of my life. Intrinsically, I'm a big believer in being authentic. I know that term is banded about a lot at the moment, but I hate photo-shopped lives – it's just not real! What you see me and my team sharing on social isn't scripted. We're sharing what's going on in our business – the downs along with the ups. As a team we have a lot of fun doing what we do but it can be difficult too. And we're happy to show both sides. That's what keeps things authentic.

Some would say corresponding with people on social media is not what CEOs/leaders should be spending their time doing. What's your view?

Bullshit. Seriously. So many people are desperately trying to leave the rat race because it can be so impersonal. People love people. So absolutely CEOs should be connecting on social media. The head of my son's school is on Twitter and he's reached out to me through that medium because he understands that's where I hang out. I dislike email and don't touch it if I can help it. I have a huge amount of respect for the head teacher in doing that. It's the same for any leader, taking the time to understand where their audiences are and then tuning in, listening and communicating what needs to be said.

Which social channels do you use and why?

Facebook is where I spend my time. I believe in owning one channel at a time.

A key barrier to getting social is 'time' – not having the time to build social properly into the work–life schedule. What are your views on this?

Social is my religion, not my tactic.

Brian J Dunn, former CEO, Best Buy

When the CEO of Best Buy, what role did social media play in your working life?

Social media acted as:

- Barometer: giving real-time feedback on public opinion... not statistically accurate but typically directionally accurate. A great way to take the consumers' temperature on any given topic relating to your business and an interesting data point on your competitors.

- Microphone: allows you to speak directly to your customers and your employees. When you can respond to consumers directly to help expedite resolution or provide explanation it goes a long way to personalizing the experience. Someone is listening. It also provides a platform to recognize business units (stores/.coms) for excellence in execution. I would frequently tweet about good store visits and market visits.

- Scout: a great place to see how new trends, technologies, strategies are taking hold. It helps you to see around corners.

How did your personal social media activity complement Best Buy's brand and campaign activity?

I did not see this as primary in how I deployed social media. For me it was about interacting with my primary constituencies, customers and employees.

What's your view about CEOs being active on social media?

Social media has allowed me to be connected in a way that was illuminating relative to trends and attitudes. An early warning system of sorts. I believe the role of the CEO is to be in touch with where the consumer meets the brand and how your employees are keeping the promise. It is also an excellent employee recognition tool. For me, being active with social media was important. Every CEO needs to pick the right tools for them but for me social media was and still is a critical set of tools.

What advice can you share about content creation/curation and day-to-day activity?

I used my social media to communicate and connect with ideas, trends and people. You need to have caution in not making it an advertising vehicle but instead the platforms can and should be a place to humanize the brand.

With millennials set to become 50 per cent of the workforce by 2020, what's your view around Snapchat/Instagram?

You need to be where your customers and employees are 'hanging out'. There is no doubt that Snapchat and Instagram – with their massive popularity – are important places to be. However, you need to be very careful that you are not just 'screaming louder' – it really is important to be yourself, authentic and not make your interactions advertisements. By your presence and actions, they can be brand accretive but you must guard against using the platforms for straight-up advertising.

Did/do you plan your social media and content creation?

Not typically. I used social media to communicate with employees and customers.

Are you/were you supported by a social media team/assistant/agency?

I had a great communications team that supported me in several areas... (video production, blogging, newsletter creation). However, my social media interactions were mine.

How much time would you say you dedicated/dedicate to social media activity?

Hard to break out, but as CEO you are never 'off duty' and I would track social media first thing in the morning and last thing at night. I travelled a great deal so it lent itself to airport time quite readily.

Many CEOs cite 'fear of saying the wrong thing' as a barrier to getting on social – what are your views around that?

I understand this and was always careful to stay away from, for example, politics and really focused my interactions on experiences that people (customers and employees) had with the brand.

Another key barrier to getting social is 'time' – not having the time to build social properly into the work–life schedule. What are your views on this?

It was and is part of my life. To me saying you don't have the time is like saying communication doesn't fit into my schedule.

What's the most challenging aspect of 'being social'?

Getting started!

What's the most rewarding aspect of 'being social'?

I made connections with people that to this day are still active and rewarding.

Do you agree that today's CEOs need to adapt quickly to social?

I agree 100 per cent. Social media platforms are going to become more prevalent, not less. I think those who ignore them do so at their peril.

What's the outlook for the next 10 years – where are we heading with social?

Social media will continue to unfold at an exponential rate. It is not going away!

What words of advice would you give to other CEOs?

It is critical to be where your customers and employees are; it will help you to understand how they feel, what they care about. Be authentic, don't be afraid to say, 'I don't know but I will find out.'

Steve Tappin, CEO, Xinfu, and host of CEO Guru

There is a body of research that indicates that being a 'social leader' has a significant and positive impact on the organization. What's your view on this?

Social leaders have a positive impact as they contribute to brand awareness and strengthening and developing relationships. The better ones get smart at using content and insight to attract value. Whilst the value of holding social connections is not easily predictable, there is clearly evidence to support that building brand awareness and developing and strengthening relationships do have a positive impact on an organization.

Do you agree that CEOs and leaders should be using social as part of their leadership/communication toolkit – and, if so, in what capacity?

Too many leaders focus internally rather than balancing external social and internal communications. My sense is that whilst the CEO is involved in creating content, connections and ideas, they need the support of a social team to best deliver the right message to the right channel.

Are you saying that you don't think that leaders and CEOs should be managing their own social media activity? One of the key themes coming through from the leaders I interviewed was the importance of the leader being 'authentic', and whilst getting support from a team with content and campaigns, the day-to-day voice needs to be that of the leader. Would you disagree with that?

No, I agree that CEOs need to have their own voice at the heart of their social media brand as well as a voice relating to the work of their team.

What's your view on having a plan? Should leaders leave social media activity to chance?

I think CEOs should have a regular game plan to cover the next four to six weeks but must also be ready to adapt to opportunities that arise.

INDEX

Note: Bold page numbers indicate figures.